Whatever Happened to the Holy Spirit?

Whatever Happened to the Holy Spirit?

by
John MacArthur, Jr.

"GRACE TO YOU"
P.O. Box 4000
Panorama City, CA   91412

Library of Congress Cataloging in Publication Data

MacArthur, John, 1939-
    Whatever happened to the Holy Spirit? / by John MacArthur, Jr.
       p.   cm. — (John MacArthur's Bible studies)
    ISBN 0-8024-5387-2
    1. Bible. N.T. Galatians—Criticism, interpretation, etc.
  2. Holy Spirit—Biblical teaching. I. Title. II. Series:
MacArthur, John, 1939-   Bible studies.
BS2685.6.H62M33   1989
231'.3—dc20   89-27216
                                                 CIP

1 2 3 4 5 6 Printing/LC/Year 93 92 91 90 89

Printed in the United States of America

Contents

1
Whatever Happened to the Holy Spirit?

Outline

Introduction
A. The Passage
B. The Problem
C. The Point

Lesson
 I. Confused Creed
   A. A Misrepresentation of the Spirit's Work
   B. An Overemphasis on the Miraculous
   C. An Unwillingness to Confront
 II. Confused Confidence
   A. The Rise of Pragmatism
   B. The Results of Pragmatism
     1. A disinterest in prayer
     2. Spiritless programming
     3. A preoccupation with church growth
     4. A decline in God-centered preaching
     5. A lack of biblical understanding
       a) Theological error
         (1) The sovereignty of God
         (2) The depravity of man
       b) Methodological error
         (1) The problem
         (2) The solution
 III. Confused Counseling
   A. Psychology: The New Approach to Problem Solving
   B. Scripture: The Final Authority for Problem Solving

Conclusion

Introduction

When I was a young man preaching around the country, I received constant requests for messages on the ministry of the Holy Spirit. Christians talked about walking in the Spirit and what it meant to be filled with the Spirit. The manifestation and use of spiritual gifts was a topic of great interest.

However, that has changed. The Holy Spirit now seems to be the forgotten member of the Trinity. Therefore the priority of the Holy Spirit in the life of the church must again be asserted. Galatians 3 does just that.

A. The Passage

In verses 1-3 the apostle Paul says, "You foolish Galatians, who has bewitched you, before whose eyes Jesus Christ was publicly portrayed as crucified? This is the only thing I want to find out from you: did you receive the Spirit by the works of the Law, or by hearing with faith? Are you so foolish? Having begun by the Spirit, are you now being perfected by the flesh?"

B. The Problem

All Christians acknowledge that life in Christ begins by the work of the Spirit. We cannot be perfected or brought to maturity through the flesh. Yet many in the church today seem to believe that we can. In Galatians 3:1-3, Paul wants his readers to understand that sanctification comes by trusting in the power of the Holy Spirit by faith. He called the Galatians foolish because they trusted in God for salvation, yet compromised the gospel of grace by relying on human effort for their personal holiness and spiritual maturity.

Paul asks in verse 1 whether the Galatians had been "bewitched" (Gk., *baskainō*, "to fascinate" or "charm someone in a misleading way"). They had been misled by people who had told them that sanctification was something they needed to accomplish on their own. The Galatians had by faith received and been empowered by the Holy Spirit, but they were becoming willing victims of a flesh-pleasing brand of sanctification.

C. The Point

If a person receives eternal salvation and the fullness of the indwelling Holy Spirit by wholeheartedly trusting in the crucified Christ, why would he trade supernatural power for human effort? That's what Paul was asking in Galatians 3. You cannot achieve a spiritual goal by natural means. The Holy Spirit initiates spiritual life, and He also sustains it.

The Holy Spirit is to the Christian what the Creator is to the creation. Without God the world would never have come into existence. And without His sustaining it, the world would go out of existence. Similarly, without the Holy Spirit none of us would ever become saved. And without His constant sanctifying, sustaining, and preserving work, the spiritual life of the Christian would drop back into the spiritual deadness whence it came. Paul said, "He who began a good work in you will perfect it until the day of Christ Jesus" (Phil. 1:6). Indeed, "we live by the Spirit" (Gal. 5:25).

In the evangelical church today, many people are attempting to perfect in the flesh what was begun by the Spirit. Systematically and subtly, the Holy Spirit is being eliminated from the matter of sanctification, and that poses a monumental threat to the church. Unless we are perfected by the Holy Spirit, all our efforts are in vain.

Lesson

I. CONFUSED CREED

A. A Misrepresentation of the Spirit's Work

The charismatic movement has contributed to the current de-emphasis of the Holy Spirit's role in sanctification by misrepresenting the ministry, baptism, filling, and illuminating work of the Spirit. That has led many believers to attempt to perfect in the flesh what was begun by the Spirit. We need to understand what the Bible teaches about the Spirit's work if we are to grow spiritually.

B. An Overemphasis on the Miraculous

A chief way that the Holy Spirit has been misrepresented is by associating Him exclusively with miracles, signs, and wonders—anything extraordinary. He is presented as the magical member of the Trinity, who moves in ways that are either seen, felt, or heard. As a result, the internal, sanctifying, purifying work that the Spirit does in the heart has been severely downplayed.

C. An Unwillingness to Confront

Many Christians are now fearful of speaking the truth for fear that someone might be offended. Therefore, there is very little talk, teaching, or preaching about the Holy Spirit anymore.

II. Confused Confidence

A. The Rise of Pragmatism

Pragmatism has replaced supernaturalism in many of today's churches, and our reliance on the Spirit has correspondingly suffered. A pseudo-Christian humanism has infiltrated the church, and we have become man-centered. That development is paralleled in history.

According to some reckonings, from about A.D. 500 to 1500 Western culture experienced what is known as the Dark Ages. The Roman Catholic church as a political and religious authority dominated Western civilization and controlled what men thought. The printing press was not invented until the end of that period, so the distribution of information was very restricted.

The Reformation changed all that. There was an explosion of independent thinking, and the chains of Rome were shattered. The invention of the printing press made large quantities of information available. People could see, study, analyze, criticize, and evaluate biblical issues and others as well. The Enlightenment caused man to move away from theological issues and focus on himself. The Industrial Revolution seemed to confirm man's brilliance through his creativity and invention. Rationalism was born out of those developments. Man began to worship his own intellect. One example of that trend is Thomas Paine's *Age of Reason*, in which the eighteenth-century political theorist debunked the Bible and exalted the human mind.

Out of rationalism came liberal theology. Theologians examined the Bible in the light of human rationality and threw out the parts they deemed irrational. Man's mind became his own standard. When man focuses on his own achievements, he turns from the supernatural to the natural. Our society is doing that now, as man's achievements far surpass those of the Enlightenment. We have witnessed tremendous progress in our time, and the result has been narcissistic self-worship. Many have come to believe that man has all the answers—a form of humanism that I call pragmatism.

B. The Results of Pragmatism

1. A disinterest in prayer

    We understand the theology of prayer, the command to pray, and the various elements of prayer. The problem is that we have come to believe that we don't need to pray. Who needs to pray for his daily bread in a society of plenty? We have developed systems to deal with practically everything. Desperate people usually don't need lectures on prayer—the ones who need to be prompted to pray are those who think they have the solution to everything.

2. Spiritless programming

    We often act as if "the weapons of our warfare are . . . of the flesh" (contrary to 2 Cor. 10:4). People who tell others that the way to solve their problems is to get in touch with themselves—rather than with the Spirit of

11

God—are using the pragmatic approach. They are attempting to solve problems by programs and methodology rather than with spiritual power.

3. A preoccupation with church growth

I am often asked what I think about church growth techniques. My standard answer is that I have absolutely no desire to build the church. That generally surprises people until I remind them that Christ said He would build the church (Matt. 16:18). I don't want to compete with Him.

When people talk about church growth, they generally mean some methodology based on human ingenuity by which the church grows. But Scripture says it is the Lord who adds to the church (Acts 2:47). Man never adds to Christ's church through his own cleverness. There is great danger when the church thinks it is rich and has need of nothing (Rev. 3:17). It is also dangerous for the church to replace supernaturalism with pragmatism, a sophisticated methodology that pretends to resolve every issue in the church, the family, and our personal lives.

4. A decline in God-centered preaching

Today's preaching reflects the pragmatic approach. So much of it is man-centered, dominated by a relational mentality that focuses on reconciling man to man, not man to God. It teaches techniques we can implement in our lives so that we can get what we want.

5. A lack of biblical understanding

a) Theological error

(1) The sovereignty of God

Pragmatism fails to understand basic theological truth. The pragmatic approach to problem solving does not account for the sovereignty of God.

Because He is sovereign, only God can solve problems.

(2) The depravity of man

Pragmatic problem solving also fails to account for the depravity of man. Man cannot solve his own problems. His only hope is to get in touch with God. Two people working together will not help each other unless God is working through one on behalf of the other.

b) Methodological error

(1) The problem

Man is a fallen creature. Human depravity is so pervasive that we cannot do anything for ourselves in the spiritual realm. Thus, the use of human means to solve spiritual problems will inevitably result in failure.

(2) The solution·

However, if you understand that God is absolutely sovereign and that man is totally depraved, you will seek supernatural solutions to your problems. The weapons of your warfare will be spiritual, not fleshly.

III. CONFUSED COUNSELING

A. Psychology: The New Approach to Problem Solving

A new approach to spiritual problem solving is what I call psychological sanctification. A product of humanism and pragmatism, psychological sanctification is the belief that deep-seated problems will be solved only by going to a counselor. The counselor supposedly helps you get in touch with your problems, and then you are supposed to reach inside yourself and dig out the answers that are within you.

Is Biblical Counseling Valid?

Absolutely! There are many wonderful people who counsel from the Word of God, intercede in prayer, and help the heavy-hearted through the Holy Spirit. The gift of exhortation is a wonderful gift by which the Holy Spirit ministers through believers to other believers. We are all called to help, stimulate, and encourage one another in the Body of Christ.

However this new definition of sanctification through psychology is neither biblical nor of the Holy Spirit. I have noticed that in many seminaries those students who might have become pastoral majors are instead choosing to major in psychology. Biblical emphasis has been replaced by an emphasis on psychology. The ministry of the Holy Spirit has been disregarded. Self-esteem, self-worth, and man-centeredness have led many to have greater confidence in their own ability than they should; they develop greater confidence in themselves than in the Holy Spirit.

B. Scripture: The Final Authority for Problem Solving

1. The Psalms—David wrestled with every imaginable problem in life. He had happy times and sad times. He wrote of experiences in his life where the pain was so deep he could hardly bear to live—as when his son Absalom tried to kill him. He suffered from horrible guilt because of his immorality and complicity in a murder. He wrestled with understanding his heart and the nature of God. Of God he said, "Holy and awesome is His name" (Ps. 111:9), whereas he said of himself, "Wash me thoroughly from my iniquity, and cleanse me from my sin" (Ps. 51:2). He told God what he felt and cried out for relief—though he admitted that God had the right to punish him. Sometimes at the end of David's psalms there is a window of hope, and sometimes there isn't. But David went to God because he understood the sovereignty of God as well as his own depravity.

2. Jeremiah 17:9-10—"The heart is more deceitful than all else and is desperately sick; who can understand it? I, the Lord, search the heart, I test the mind." In verse 10 we see "heart" and "mind" used interchangeably,

which means our capacity to think, our ability to analyze, and our competence for evaluation are all deceitful. Problem solving by self-examination results in deceitful answers. Our sinful natures bias us in our favor against God and lie to us about what we are really like. They exalt us in our own eyes and absolve us of responsibility for sin. The answer to Jeremiah's rhetorical question, "Who can understand it?" is found in verse 10: "I, the Lord."

3. 1 Corinthians 4:4—Paul said, "I am conscious of nothing against myself, yet I am not by this acquitted; but the one who examines me is the Lord." Paul didn't know of anything against himself, but he knew he couldn't rely on that.

4. Proverbs 16:2—"All the ways of a man are clean in his own sight, but the Lord weighs the motives."

5. Proverbs 14:12—"There is a way which seems right to a man, but its end is the way of death." When we reach down inside ourselves to get answers, we only get lies. That's why we have to depend upon the Holy Spirit and not on ourselves.

Who Are We Kidding?

Why do we substitute therapists for the Holy Spirit? We may reason that if we can't trust ourselves, perhaps we can trust other men. But if we can't get the truth out of our own hearts, how will another man, who also has a deceitful heart, be able to help? We can fool a therapist the same way we fool ourselves. While we sit trying to discover what's inside of us, our hearts tell us lies. Can we expect a therapist to discern the truth from the lies we are telling him and then be able to tell us what we ought to do with our deceitful hearts? Who are we kidding?

6. Psalm 7:9—"Let the evil of the wicked come to an end, but establish the righteous; for the righteous, God tries the hearts and minds." Only God can test, evaluate, and know the truth of a man's heart.

7. Psalm 26:2—"Examine me, O Lord, and try me; test my mind and my heart." David didn't want a human counselor. He turned to God and wrestled in prayer. He was repentant, broken, and contrite.

8. Psalm 139:1-7—"O Lord, Thou hast searched me and known me. Thou dost know when I sit down and when I rise up; Thou dost understand my thought from afar. Thou dost scrutinize my path and my lying down, and art intimately acquainted with all my ways. Even before there is a word on my tongue, behold, O Lord, Thou dost know it all. Thou hast enclosed me behind and before, and laid Thy hand upon me. Such knowledge is too wonderful for me; it is too high, I cannot attain to it. Where can I go from Thy Spirit?" God isn't misled by skewed signals—He knows everything about you. If you want to get in touch with "the real you," get in touch with the Spirit.

9. Psalm 32:6-8—"Let everyone who is godly pray to Thee in a time when Thou mayest be found; surely in a flood of great waters they shall not reach him. Thou art my hiding place; Thou dost preserve me from trouble; Thou dost surround me with songs of deliverance. I will instruct you and teach you in the way which you should go; I will counsel you with My eye upon you." Before trouble occurs, the godly pray to God, and in the midst of trouble they turn to Him. They are assured of deliverance, instruction, and counsel from God. If you want accountability, only God can give it absolutely. If you want counsel, only God will give you advice you can fully trust.

10. 1 Corinthians 2:12—"We have received, not the spirit of the world, but the Spirit who is from God, that we might know the things freely given to us by God." The Holy Spirit is the source of our supernatural resources. When we want to know the truth about ourselves and the solutions to our problems, we need to go to the Holy Spirit.

11. Job 12:13—"With Him [God] are wisdom and might; to Him belong counsel and understanding." We substitute human counsel for God's truth because we believe

we can solve our problems through our own cleverness, ingenuity, and systems. But that is to substitute our own abilities for the Spirit's power.

12. Job 12:17-20—"He [God] makes counselors walk barefoot" He strips them—"and makes fools of judges. He loosens the bond of kings, and binds their loins with a girdle. He makes priests walk barefoot, and overthrows the secure ones. He deprives the trusted ones of speech, and takes away the discernment of the elders." The wisdom of God is so far beyond man's that the greatest counselors are stripped naked before God's glory.

13. Job 12:24-25—"He deprives of intelligence the chiefs of the earth's people, and makes them wander in a pathless waste. They grope in darkness with no light, and He makes them stagger like a drunken man."

Conclusion

Our counselor must be God. The great tragedy of the church today is that it is filled with sin and weakness—a situation that will continue to get worse until we realize that spiritual warfare is fought with spiritual weapons. Techniques, theories, and therapies will never restrain the flesh because they appeal to the flesh. Solutions to personal, family, and church problems are found in God's counsel ministered through the Spirit of God. We must turn to the Spirit of God, learn to walk in the Spirit, and understand the power of the Spirit. We must reject man-centered, humanistic, psychological solutions to problems. Built into those solutions are false impressions of man's ability, which create the illusion of sanctification by intellectual achievement. The Galatians tried to perfect in the flesh what had begun in the Spirit, but it was a faulty solution then and it is a faulty solution now.

Focusing on the Facts

1. According to Paul, how is sanctification accomplished in the life of a believer (see p. 8)?

2. What led Paul to ask if the Galatian church had been "bewitched" (see pp. 8-9)?
3. What does it mean when we say that the Holy Spirit is to the Christian what God as Creator is to the creation (Gal. 3:1; see p. 9)?
4. What monumental threat faces the evangelical church today (see p. 9)?
5. What movement has led to the practical elimination of the scriptural emphasis on the internal sanctifying work of the Spirit? How did that happen (see pp. 9-10)?
6. Instead of reliance on the supernatural power of the Holy Spirit, what philosophy of problem solving has infiltrated the church today (see p. 10)?
7. What did Thomas Paine do in his *The Age of Reason* (see p. 11)?
8. What happens to the prayer life of a self-reliant Christian (see p. 11)?
9. How does church growth occur, according to the New Testament (see p. 12)?
10. What two theological errors does the pragmatic approach make? Explain each (see pp. 12-13).
11. Psychological sanctification promotes self-esteem, self-worth, and self-centeredness. What happens to our reliance on the Holy Spirit when we accept such systems of thought (p. 14)?
12. Where are the answers to man's problems found? Support your answer with Scripture (see pp. 14-17).

Pondering the Principles

1. Dr. Martyn Lloyd-Jones summed up the plight of man in this way: "Man believes in his own mind and his own understanding, and the greatest insult that can ever be offered to him is to tell him, as Christ tells him, that he must become as a little child and be born again" (*The Plight of Man and the Power of God* [Grand Rapids: Baker, 1982], p. 23). Paul asked the "foolish" Galatians if they thought they could perfect in the flesh what was begun in the Spirit (Galatians 3:3). If man's plight is so bad prior to conversion, what effect will self-reliant strategies for spiritual growth have on those who profess conversion? On what or whom do you rely as your guide for spiritual growth?

2. In John Bunyan's *The Pilgrim's Progress*, the character Shameful says that it is "a pitiful, low, shameful business for a person to surrender his will and life to become a servant of [Christ]; that a tender conscience was an unmanly weakness; and that for a person to watch over his own words, attitude, and conduct, tying himself down to rules that destroyed his liberty . . . would make him the ridicule and laughingstock of present-day society" (*Pilgrim's Progress in Today's English*, James H. Thomas, ed. [Chicago: Moody, 1964], pp. 73-74). Many in the church today agree with Shameful and promote the idea that the fundamental problem with mankind is lack of self-esteem. However, Jesus said, "The greatest among you shall be your servant. And whoever exalts himself shall be humbled; and whoever humbles himself shall be exalted" (Matt. 23:11-12). Where is your sense of worth centered—in yourself or in Christ? What effect does your answer have on a true sense of self-worth?

2
The Ministries of the Holy Spirit—Part 1

Outline

Introduction

Review

Lesson
A. The Holy Spirit Is the Agent of Salvation
   1. He produces conviction
   2. He produces repentance
   3. He empowers preaching
   4. He regenerates hearts
B. The Holy Spirit Is the Agent of Sanctification
   1. He indwells believers
   2. He baptizes believers into the Body of Christ
   3. He gives spiritual gifts to believers
   4. He secures every believer's eternal inheritance
   5. He sanctifies believers
I. The Holy Spirit Provides Access to God
  A. The Significance of Access to God
  B. The Illustration of Access to God
  C. The Means of Access to God
   1. From a negative perspective
   2. From a positive perspective
  D. The Benefits of Access to God
   1. We have fellowship with God
   2. We have resources for every need
   3. We have wisdom for every circumstance

II. The Holy Spirit Illuminates Scripture
   A. Illumination Defined
   B. Illumination Illustrated

Conclusion

Introduction

In Galatians 3:1-5 Paul says, "You foolish Galatians, who has bewitched you, before whose eyes Jesus Christ was publicly portrayed as crucified? This is the only thing I want to find out from you: did you receive the Spirit by the works of the Law, or by hearing with faith? Are you so foolish? Having begun by the Spirit, are you now being perfected by the flesh? Did you suffer so many things in vain—if indeed it was in vain? Does He then, who provides you with the Spirit and works miracles among you, do it by the works of the Law, or by hearing with faith?"

Paul was reminding the Galatian believers that the Christian life begins by the power of the Holy Spirit through faith, and it must continue that way. They could not reach spiritual maturity by human efforts apart from the Spirit's power. I think most Christians today would agree with that principle, yet we are facing a new form of Galatianism: an attempt to be sanctified by works apart from God's Spirit.

Review

We have seen several reasons for the church's defection from true sanctification: the confused creed resulting from the charismatic movement (see pp. 9-10), the confused confidence resulting from pragmatism (see pp. 10-13), and the confused counseling resulting from overdependence on psychology (see pp. 13-17). A misunderstanding of the depravity of man and the sovereignty of God is at the heart of the matter (see pp. 12-13).

Many people believe that if a man is offered the right program or theory he can somehow change himself. But that belief betrays a

misunderstanding of the depravity of man. We can't sanctify ourselves any more than we can save ourselves. Only God saves and
sanctifies by His Spirit through faith. Yet after being saved by the
Spirit, Christians often depend on human psychology rather than
on the Holy Spirit to solve their problems and define standards of
behavior. But sanctification apart from the Holy Spirit is not sanctification at all.

False sanctification is a serious problem, but the solution is simple:
we must depend on the Holy Spirit for sanctification just as we depended on Him for salvation.

Lesson

Scripture reveals the comprehensive nature of the Spirit's ministry
in the believer's life.

A. The Holy Spirit Is the Agent of Salvation

There are four aspects of His saving work.

1. He produces conviction

Jesus spoke of the Spirit's convicting the world of sin
(John 16:8). Conviction is an awareness of guilt regarding
one's own sins. Only God can produce that awareness.
He uses believers to proclaim His truth about sin, but the
Spirit must apply the truth to unbelieving men and
women's hearts to produce conviction. Without the
work of the Spirit, they would continue to deny their sinfulness and their need for a Savior.

2. He produces repentance

Repentance is a desire to turn from our sins once we
have been convicted of them. God grants repentance
(2 Tim. 2:25) because men are incapable of repenting on
their own. They love darkness more than light (John
3:19). Acts 11:18 says, "God has granted to the Gentiles . . . the repentance that leads to life."

3. He empowers preaching

The Spirit empowers God's truth so that it penetrates the unbeliever's mind and begins to do its saving work. He empowers both the preacher and the hearer. Both works of the Spirit are necessary for effective proclamation and reception of divine truth (1 Thess. 2:13). First Peter 1:12 speaks of "those who preached the gospel . . . by the Holy Spirit," and 1 John 5:7 says, "It is the Spirit who bears witness, because the Spirit is the truth." The Spirit's power is the key element in effective preaching.

4. He regenerates hearts

Jesus said to Nicodemus, " 'Unless one is born again, he cannot see the kingdom of God.' Nicodemus said to Him, 'How can a man be born when he is old? He cannot enter a second time into his mother's womb and be born, can he?' Jesus answered, 'Truly, truly, I say to you, unless one is born of water and the Spirit, he cannot enter into the kingdom of God. That which is born of the flesh is flesh and that which is born of the Spirit is spirit. Do not marvel that I said to you, "You must be born again." The wind blows where it wishes and you hear the sound of it, but do not know where it comes from and where it is going; so is everyone who is born of the Spirit' " (John 3:3-8).

Paul said, "He saved us, not on the basis of deeds which we have done in righteousness, but according to His mercy, by the washing of regeneration and renewing by the Holy Spirit, whom He poured out" (Titus 3:5-6).

Which Method of Evangelism Is Best?

Since salvation is a supernatural work, the issue is not what method you use to present the gospel. However, it is of major consequence that you present the gospel accurately and in the power of the Holy Spirit. Methods of evangelism alone can't convince someone to repent and turn to Christ. Only God can do that by applying His truth to the person's heart. Your task is to faithfully proclaim His truth and be sensitive to His Spirit's leading. Are you doing that?

B. The Holy Spirit Is the Agent of Sanctification

In addition to the initial work of conviction, repentance, and regeneration, the Spirit provides for the believer's on-going sanctification.

1. He indwells believers

At the moment of salvation the Holy Spirit takes up residence in the believer's heart.

a) Acts 2:38—Peter said, "Repent, and let each of you be baptized in the name of Jesus Christ for the forgiveness of your sins; and you shall receive the gift of the Holy Spirit."

b) 1 Corinthians 12:13—Paul said, "By one Spirit we were all baptized into one body . . . we were all made to drink of one Spirit."

c) Romans 8:9—Paul said, "You are not in the flesh but in the Spirit. . . . If anyone does not have the Spirit of Christ, he does not belong to Him."

d) 1 Corinthians 6:19—Paul said, "Your body is a temple of the Holy Spirit who is in you, whom you have from God."

2. He baptizes believers into the Body of Christ

The "Body of Christ" is a metaphor Paul used for the true church. Christ is its Head, and individual believers are its various parts. Believers become part of the Body of Christ at the moment of their salvation (1 Cor. 12:13).

3. He gives spiritual gifts to believers

Spiritual gifts allow us to do spiritual service such as preaching, teaching, governing, faith, helps, and many others. Each believer has a unique combination of gifts especially suited to him or her by the Holy Spirit. In that sense believers are like spiritual snowflakes—no two are alike. Each has a unique and important role to play within the church.

4. He secures every believer's eternal inheritance

Ephesians 1:13-14 says, "You were sealed in Him with the Holy Spirit of promise, who is given as a pledge of our inheritance." The Greek word translated "sealed" speaks of authenticity—an unbreakable promise. The Holy Spirit secures you for eternity.

The Greek word translated "pledge" (*arrabōn*) speaks of a down payment made to secure a purchase. The moment you were saved, the Spirit of God became the down payment on God's final installment of your eternal glory. In modern Greek, *arrabōn* includes the idea of an engagement ring. In that sense we can view the Holy Spirit as God's engagement ring—a sign of His deep love and His guarantee to keep His promises.

5. He sanctifies believers

Second Thessalonians 2:13 says, "God has chosen you from the beginning for salvation through sanctification by the Spirit and faith in the truth." In that context "sanctification" means we have been set apart from sin and eternal death. That is positional sanctification resulting from our standing as believers in Christ. Our practical sanctification comes as the Spirit does His transforming work within us day by day (2 Cor. 3:18).

The Christian life begins in the power of the Spirit and includes all those aspects of His supernatural work within us. That's why we should never attempt to reach spiritual maturity by human means apart from His power. Instead, we must draw from the ongoing resources He provides for our sanctification.

I. THE HOLY SPIRIT PROVIDES ACCESS TO GOD

Access to God implies intimacy with God. That means believers can approach God on a personal basis without fear of rejection.

A. The Significance of Access to God

God is the provider of all spiritual resources. Because we as Christians live on a spiritual level, our deepest needs can't be satisfied by natural commodities. Only God can satisfy those needs, and He's available to us through the Holy Spirit.

B. The Illustration of Access to God

Paul said that God sent Christ "that we might receive the adoption as sons. And because you are sons, God has sent forth the Spirit of His Son into our hearts, crying, 'Abba! Father!' Therefore you are no longer a slave, but a son; and if a son, then an heir through God . . . you have come to know God, or rather to be known by God" (Gal. 4:5-9).

We are sons of God, and sonship involves access and intimacy. The phrase "Abba! Father!" (v. 6) is a term of endearment. "Abba" can be translated "Papa" or "Daddy." It signifies family, privilege, love, and approachability. It's what the writer of Hebrews had in mind when he said, "Let us draw near with a sincere heart in full assurance of faith" (Heb. 10:22).

Paul emphasizes the same truth in Romans 8:14-16: "All who are being led by the Spirit of God, these are sons of God. For you have not received a spirit of slavery leading to fear again, but you have received a spirit of adoption as sons by which we cry out, 'Abba! Father!' The Spirit Himself bears witness with our spirit that we are children of God."

C. The Means of Access to God

1. From a negative perspective

Through prayer we have direct access to God. He's always available and approachable, yet many Christians look elsewhere to have their needs met. Often they seem willing to substitute almost anything for prayer. That might be understandable if God weren't accessible, but He is. The problem is their apparent unwillingness to pray with intensity and to wrestle with God over the issues of life.

2. From a positive perspective

a) Psalm 16:11—The psalmist wrote, "Thou wilt make known to me the path of life; in Thy presence is fulness of joy; in Thy right hand there are pleasures forever." If you want joy, pleasure, and insights into life, you can find them in His presence. You don't need to look elsewhere.

b) Psalm 27:4—David said, "One thing I have asked from the Lord, that I shall seek: that I may dwell in the house of the Lord all the days of my life, to behold the beauty of the Lord, and to meditate in His temple." That is a focused prayer that reflects David's longing to be in God's presence.

c) Psalm 42:1-3, 5-7, 9-11—The psalmist cried out to God, saying, "As the deer pants for the water brooks, so my soul pants for Thee, O God. My soul thirsts for God, for the living God; when shall I come and appear before God? My tears have been my food day and night. . . . Why are you in despair, O my soul? And why have you become disturbed within me? . . . My soul is in despair within me. . . . All Thy breakers and Thy waves have rolled over me. . . . I will say to God my rock, 'Why hast Thou forgotten me?' . . . Why are you in despair, O my soul?" That is a man who was obviously in deep despair. Note that his solution was to seek after God.

d) Psalm 73:25-26—Asaph said, "Whom have I in heaven but Thee? And besides Thee, I desire nothing on earth" (v. 25). He understood that earthly resources couldn't satisfy spiritual needs.

When Christians experience spiritual defeat it's often because they've forgotten that God alone is the source of spiritual power. Christian programs, seminars, and counseling techniques may be helpful to a point, but they can't replace the spiritual power that comes from prolonged periods of deep communion with the living God. That is our lifeline and our true source of strength.

Asaph looked to God alone for his spiritual strength. In verse 26 he says, "My flesh and my heart may fail, but God is the strength of my heart and my portion forever." Every believer can have that confidence because God's strength is available through the Holy Spirit. What a tremendous promise!

D. The Benefits of Access to God

1. We have fellowship with God

A Christian is someone who loves God (Matt. 22:37). As lovers of God we should long for fellowship and communion with Him. As we pursue that fellowship, we experience the freshness and exhilaration only He can give to our spirits; and we receive all the provisions we need for a healthy, victorious Christian life.

I've found that most people who come to me for counseling simply need a sympathetic ear and an encouraging word from Scripture. I understand the need to bear one another's burdens (Gal. 6:2) and am happy to share in that ministry, but I also think we can short-circuit the Spirit's ministry by turning to men before we turn to God. If someone feels better after simply talking to me, imagine how he would feel if he talked to God!

2. We have resources for every need

Jesus said, "Give us this day our daily bread. . . . Do not lead us into temptation" (Matt. 6:11, 13). Paul said, "My God shall supply all your needs according to His riches in glory in Christ Jesus" (Phil. 4:19). God can meet every human need.

3. We have wisdom for every circumstance

James said, "If any of you lacks wisdom, let him ask of God, who gives to all men generously and without reproach, and it will be given to him" (James 1:5).

We must never try to perfect what was begun by the Spirit of God by using the systems of man. Such efforts are unnecessary and fruitless because we have access to God Himself, who graciously gives us all the resources and wisdom we need to live according to His will.

II. THE HOLY SPIRIT ILLUMINATES SCRIPTURE

A. Illumination Defined

Having intimacy with God is wonderful, but it must be a two-way conversation: we speak to Him in prayer, and He speaks to us through His Word. Illumination is the ministry of the Spirit whereby He opens our minds to God's Word and makes it come alive to us as God speaks through its pages. That's why we should always pray with an open heart and an open Bible.

B. Illumination Illustrated

1. 1 John 2:20, 27—John said, "You have an anointing from the Holy One, and you all know [truth]. . . . The anointing which you received from Him abides in you, and you have no need for anyone to teach you; but as His anointing teaches you about all things, and is true and is not a lie, and just as it has taught you, you abide in Him." The Holy Spirit abides within every believer as the resident Truth Teacher.

   The Greek word translated "anointing" (*chrisma*) literally means "ointment" or "anointing oil." An ointment is placed onto and absorbed into one's skin. John's analogy pictures the Spirit as the One who resides within the believer and permeates his life with God's truth.

2. 2 Corinthians 1:21—Paul said, "He who establishes us with you in Christ and anointed us is God, who also sealed us and gave us the Spirit in our hearts as a pledge."

3. 1 Corinthians 2:9-14—Paul said, "Things which eye has not seen and ear has not heard, and which have not entered the heart of man, all that God has prepared for those who love Him. For to us God revealed them through the Spirit; for the Spirit searches all things, even the depths of God. For who among men knows the thoughts of a man except the spirit of the man, which is in him? Even so the thoughts of God no one knows except the Spirit of God.

"Now we have received, not the spirit of the world, but the Spirit who is from God, that we might know the things freely given to us by God, which things we also speak, not in words taught by human wisdom, but in those taught by the Spirit, combining spiritual thoughts with spiritual words. But a natural man does not accept the things of the Spirit of God."

The Spirit enables the believer to understand Scripture. He is able to do that because He is the author of Scripture. Second Peter 1:20-21 says, "No prophecy of Scripture is a matter of one's own interpretation, for no prophecy was ever made by an act of human will, but men moved by the Holy Spirit spoke from God."

To illustrate the Holy Spirit's unique qualification for revealing the Word, Paul compared the Spirit's knowledge of God's mind to a man's knowledge of his own mind (1 Cor. 2:11). God's Spirit knew God's thoughts and revealed them in Scripture. Also He illuminates those thoughts in the minds of believers (1 Cor. 2:12).

If God's Spirit Is Sufficient, Why Do We Need God's Word?

The sufficiency of God's Spirit in meeting our needs does not mean we can neglect God's Word. Quite the contrary. The Spirit works through the Word to accomplish God's purposes in our lives. PG

In my opinion Psalm 19:7-9 is the single greatest treatment of the sufficiency of Scripture in the Bible: "The law of the Lord is perfect, restoring the soul [transforming the whole person]; the testimony of the Lord is sure, making wise the simple [imparting skills for every aspect of daily living]. The precepts of the Lord are right [they establish a right path to follow], rejoicing the heart; the commandment of the Lord is pure, enlightening the eyes [enabling the believer to see truth clearly]. The fear of the Lord is clean [untouched by sin], enduring forever; the judgments of the Lord are true; they are righteous altogether."

In that passage David used six synonyms to describe Scripture: law, testimony, precepts, commandment, fear, and judgments. "Law" refers to God's standards for man's conduct. "Testimony" refers to His self-disclosure. "Precepts" refers to life principles. "Commandment" refers to non-negotiable demands. "Fear" refers to instruction on worship. And "judgments" refers to God's verdicts on man's behavior.

Scripture is sufficient to supply all God wants us to know about Himself and His will for our lives. But Scripture must be illuminated by the Holy Spirit if we are to understand it. God's Spirit working through God's Word provides a supernatural resource that exceeds anything conceivable on the natural plane. That's why Scripture is "more desirable than gold, yes, than much fine gold; sweeter also than honey and the drippings of the honeycomb" (v. 10).

David prayed, "Let the words of my mouth and the meditation of my heart be acceptable in Thy sight, O Lord, my rock and my Redeemer" (v. 14). Is that your prayer? It will be answered only when you follow the command of Joshua 1:8: "This book of the law shall not depart from your mouth, but you shall meditate on it day and night, so that you may be careful to do according to all that is written in it."

Conclusion

When we became Christians, God's Spirit convicted us of our sins, brought us to repentance, and regenerated us. He then indwelt, baptized, sealed, gifted, and separated us from sin. In the ongoing process of sanctification, He gives us access to God, who supplies all the resources we need for physical and spiritual life. The Spirit also illuminates our understanding of God's Word so that we are transformed by its principles as He applies them to our lives.

What unimaginable gifts the Spirit has given us! We are not left to flounder around seeking solutions to spiritual needs on the natural plane. God's Spirit is sufficient for every need. It is our responsibility to be filled with the Spirit and to walk by the Spirit each day (Eph. 5:18; Gal. 5:16, 25).

It is necessary to be reminded of those basic truths because we often forget the source of our spiritual power. Many Christians have been drawn away from depending upon the Spirit's ministry, focusing instead on some supposed fast answer, quick fix, or panacea for their problems. But the truth is, if you want a godly life, you must move into the presence of God through prayer and allow His Spirit to minister to you and transform you through His Word. That is how sanctification takes place.

Focusing on the Facts

1. We are facing a new form of Galatianism: an attempt to be _____ by _____ apart from God's Spirit (see p. 22).
2. What are four aspects of the Spirit's saving work (see pp. 23-24)?
3. Define *conviction* (see p. 23).
4. Define *repentance* (see p. 23).
5. According to Acts 11:18, who grants repentance (see p. 23)?
6. The _____ _____ is the key element in effective preaching (see p. 24).
7. What is your task in evangelism (see p. 24)?
8. What are five ways in which the Spirit provides for the believer's ongoing sanctification (see pp. 25-26)?
9. What did Paul mean by the Body of Christ (1 Cor. 12:13; see p. 25)?
10. What is a spiritual gift (see p. 25)?
11. Define *arrabōn* as used in Ephesians 1:14 (see p. 26).
12. Access to God implies _____ with God (see p. 26).
13. What is the significance of having access to God (see p. 26)?
14. What does the expression "Abba! Father!" mean (Gal. 4:6; see p. 27)?
15. What is the means of access to God (see pp. 27-28)?
16. What was Asaph's perspective on the ability of earthly resources to satisfy spiritual needs (Ps. 73:25-26; see pp. 28-29)?
17. What are three benefits of having access to God (see p. 29)?
18. Define *illumination* (see p. 30).
19. Does the sufficiency of the Spirit diminish our need for God's Word? Explain (see p. 31).
20. What titles did David use to describe God's Word? What does each title mean (Ps. 19:7-9; see pp. 31-32)?

Pondering the Principles

1. We have seen that every believer has direct access to God through the Holy Spirit and prayer. That's how we cultivate intimacy and fellowship with Him. What a tremendous privilege! Do you take advantage of your access to God? Don't let complacency or neglect rob you of the spiritual power and refreshment that comes from time spent in His presence. There is no substitute for prayer. If you have not developed a systematic approach to prayer, the "ACTS" format is a good way to start.

   - Adoration—praising God
   - Confession—confessing sin
   - Thanksgiving—thanking God
   - Supplication—praying for others

   Whatever approach you use, be faithful and disciplined in prayer. It honors God and is your lifeline to a victorious Christian life.

2. Illumination is the ministry of the Spirit whereby He opens our minds to God's Word and makes it come alive to us. As we communicate with God in prayer, He communicates with us through His Word. That is where we find God's answers to our questions and His solutions to our problems. Other sources of information, such as seminars and counseling, are helpful only to the degree that they are consistent with God's Word. Therefore, our first source of instruction and the standard by which we should measure all others must be God's Word. Is that the standard you use? Are you discerning about what you listen to and whose advice you follow?

3
The Ministries of the Holy Spirit—Part 2

Outline

Introduction
A. The Purpose
B. The Passage
C. The Problem
   1. As confronted by Paul
   2. As illustrated by Joseph Carroll
D. The Provision
E. The Pattern
   1. The example of St. Augustine the theologian
   2. The example of Asaph the psalmist
   3. The example of Hudson Taylor the missionary

Review
 I. The Holy Spirit Provides Access to God
II. The Holy Spirit Illuminates Scripture

Lesson
III. The Holy Spirit Glorifies Christ
   A. As Explained by Jesus
   B. As Explained by Paul
IV. The Holy Spirit Guides Believers
   A. As Explained by Ezekiel
   B. As Explained by David
   C. As Explained by Luke
   D. As Explained by Paul
   E. As Explained by A. W. Pink

Conclusion

Introduction

A. The Purpose

The purpose of this study is to call Christians back to living on the spiritual plane. Somehow many Christians have drifted away from believing in the sufficiency of the Holy Spirit for all matters of Christian living. Instead they have substituted all kinds of earthly things for His supernatural power. My earnest desire is to see Christians return to depending on the power of God's Spirit, so they will know the joy and victory that only He can give.

B. The Passage

In Galatians 3:1-5 Paul says, "You foolish Galatians, who has bewitched you, before whose eyes Jesus Christ was publicly portrayed as crucified? This is the only thing I want to find out from you: did you receive the Spirit by the works of the Law, or by hearing with faith? Are you so foolish? Having begun by the Spirit, are you now being perfected by the flesh? Did you suffer so many things in vain—if indeed it was in vain? Does He then, who provides you with the Spirit and works miracles among you, do it by the works of the Law, or by hearing with faith?"

C. The Problem

1. As confronted by Paul

The Galatian believers had been saved by the power of God's Spirit but were attempting to be sanctified by their own efforts. Paul confronted the folly of their thinking by reminding them that what had been begun by the Spirit couldn't be sustained by human effort.

His indictment was direct because the issue was serious. And I believe it to be a timeless indictment that relates directly to us. Obviously our culture and specific circumstances are different, but the problem of attempting to perfect in the flesh what was begun in the Spirit remains the same.

2. As illustrated by Joseph Carroll

I recently heard pastor Joseph Carroll tell about an experience he had that illustrates this point. He was conducting a series of meetings in both North and South Carolina; during that campaign he stayed in the home of close friends in Asheville and traveled each night to his various speaking engagements.

One night he was scheduled to speak at a church in Greenville, South Carolina, which is several hours from Asheville. Because he didn't have a car, some folks from Greenville volunteered to transport him to and from the meeting. When they arrived to pick him up, he said farewell to his hosts and told them he hoped to be back by midnight or soon afterward.

After ministering at the Greenville church, he stayed for a while to enjoy some fellowship and then rode back to Asheville. As he approached the house, he saw the porch light on and assumed his hosts were prepared for his arrival, since he had discussed the time of his return with them. As he got out of the car, he sent his driver on his way, saying, "You must hurry. You have a long drive back. I'm sure they're prepared for me; I'll have no problem."

He felt the bitter cold of the winter night as he walked the long distance to the house. By the time he reached the porch, his nose and ears were numb. He tapped gently on the door, but no one answered. He tapped a little harder and then even harder, but still there was no reply. Finally, in a bit of a concern about the cold, he tapped on the kitchen door and on a side window but there was no response.

Somewhat frustrated and growing colder by the moment, he decided to walk to a neighboring house so that he could call and awaken his hosts. Then he realized that knocking on someone's door after midnight wasn't a safe thing to do, so he decided to find a public telephone. It was very dark and cold, and he wasn't familiar with the area. Consequently, he walked for several miles. At one point he slipped as he walked in wet grass growing on the bank along the road and slid down into two feet of water. Soaked and nearly frozen, he crawled back up to the road and walked further until he finally saw a blinking motel light. He awakened the motel manager, who was gracious enough to let him use the phone.

He made the call and said to his sleepy host, "I hate to disturb you, but I couldn't get anyone to wake up in the house. I'm several miles down the road at the motel. Could you come get me?" To which his host replied, "Joseph, you have a key in your overcoat pocket. I gave it to you before you left." Sure enough, he reached into his pocket, and there was the key.

That story is a picture of many Christians. They want access to the house of blessing. They want comfort, warmth, rest, peace, nourishment, and fellowship. And they try a variety of human schemes to get in—all of which are unsuccessful. Yet all the while they possess the key: the Holy Spirit. He alone can relieve their frustrations and fulfill the deepest longings of their hearts.

How have so many Christians been deceived into thinking they can gain entrance into the house of blessing by relying on pragmatism, psychotherapy, and other human means, when Scripture clearly teaches that the Holy Spirit is the key to God's provision?

D. The Provision

(God provides everything we need for life and godliness. We need only turn to Him.)

1. Psalm 23:1-6

Psalm 23 illustrates the sufficiency of God's provision to believers: "The Lord is my shepherd, I shall not want" (v. 1). I can go to God for anything I lack, and He will supply my needs. If I need food or water, "He makes me lie down in green pastures; He leads me beside quiet waters" (v. 2). Similarly, if my soul is weak and weary, "he restores my soul" (v. 3). If I'm lost and don't know

38

how to chart the course of my life, "He guides me in the paths of righteousness for His name's sake" (v. 3). Someday I will have to face the reality of death, but "even though I walk through the valley of the shadow of death, I fear no evil; for Thou art with me" (v. 4). I am often distressed and in upheaval, but "Thy rod and Thy staff, they comfort me" (v. 4). I am concerned about those around me who are hostile, but "Thou dost prepare a table before me in the presence of my enemies" (v. 5). I need healing, so "Thou hast anointed my head with oil" (v. 5). It's a long life and I want to make the best of it, so He makes "my cup [overflow]. Surely goodness and lovingkindness will follow me all the days of my life" (vv. 5-6). And I desperately want hope after death, so He promises that "I will dwell in the house of the Lord forever" (v. 6).

Our Shepherd graciously supplies everything we need. Why would we go anywhere else?

2. Colossians 2:10

Paul said, "In [Christ] you have been made complete."

3. Ephesians 1:3

God "has blessed us with every spiritual blessing in the heavenly places in Christ."

4. Philippians 4:13, 19

Paul said, "I can do all things through Him who strengthens me. . . . My God shall supply all your needs according to His riches in glory in Christ Jesus."

5. 2 Peter 1:3

Christ "has granted to us everything pertaining to life and godliness."

Can it be that we have forgotten those provisions? How else can we account for so many Christians attempting to satisfy spiritual needs by human means? Paul said that all such attempts are foolish (Gal. 3:3). Why then do we continue to fall prey to our own inabilities? That only increases our frustration as we realize we can't solve our problems apart from God's Spirit.

E. The Pattern

Every issue of life that a Christian faces can be resolved in the power and presence of God. That truth has been the foundation of spiritual commitment for centuries. Throughout the history of the church, the greatest men of God have been men of prayer, striving for intimate communion with God. They knew that the Christian life, which begins in the Spirit, could only be sustained by the Spirit.

1. The example of St. Augustine the theologian

St. Augustine prayed in his *Confessions*, "Hide not Thy face from me. Oh! That I might repose on Thee. Oh! That Thou wouldest enter into my heart and inebriate it, that I may forget my ills and embrace Thee, my sole good."

2. The example of Asaph the psalmist

In Psalm 73:25 he declares, "Whom have I in heaven but Thee? And besides Thee, I desire nothing on earth."

3. The example of Hudson Taylor the missionary

Taylor's son wrote, "Frequently those who were wakeful in the little house at Chinkiang [in China] might hear, at two or three in the morning, the soft refrain of Mr. Taylor's favorite hymn [Jesus, I am resting, resting, in the joy of what Thou art . . .]. He had learned that for him, only one life was possible—just that blessed life of resting and rejoicing in the Lord under all circumstances, while He dealt with the difficulties, inward and outward, great and small" (Dr. Howard Taylor, *Hudson Taylor's Spiritual Secret* [Chicago: Moody, 1932], p. 209).

Dr. Taylor also recorded a journal entry showing how his father dealt with grief and loneliness following his first wife's death: "How lonesome . . . were the weary hours when confined to my room. How I missed my dear wife. . . . The Lord had made [this] passage so real to me, 'Whosoever drinketh of the water that I shall give him shall never thirst.' Twenty times a day, perhaps, as I felt the heart-thirst coming back, I cried to Him: 'Lord, you promised! You promised me that I should never thirst.' And whether I called by day or night, how quickly He always came and satisfied my sorrowing heart! So much so that I often wondered whether it were possible that my loved one who had been taken could be enjoying more of His presence than I was in my lonely chamber" (*Hudson Taylor and the China Inland Mission: The Growth of a Work of God* [London: Religious Tract Society, 1940], p. 200).

Review

We have seen that the Christian life begins when the Holy Spirit brings conviction, repentance, and regeneration (see pp. 23-24). He also indwells, baptizes, gifts, secures, and separates the believer from sin and death (see pp. 25-26). That is how believers begin in the Spirit, and they will be perfected in the Spirit by means of His sanctifying work.

I. THE HOLY SPIRIT PROVIDES ACCESS TO GOD (see pp. 26-29)

II. THE HOLY SPIRIT ILLUMINATES SCRIPTURE (see pp. 30-31)

Lesson

III. THE HOLY SPIRIT GLORIFIES CHRIST

The Spirit glorifies Christ by revealing His majesty and glory in Scripture and by producing Christ-centered lives in believers. A life that is focused on knowing, loving, obeying, and serving Christ brings honor to Him by displaying His characteristics to the watching world (Matt. 5:16).

A. As Explained by Jesus

1. John 15:26

   Jesus said, "When the Helper [the Holy Spirit] comes, whom I will send to you from the Father . . . He will bear witness of Me." The Spirit bears witness of Christ by revealing His glory.

2. John 16:13-15

   Jesus also said, "When He, the Spirit of Truth, comes . . . He shall glorify Me; for He shall take of Mine, and shall disclose it to you. All things that the Father has are Mine; therefore I said, that He takes of Mine, and will disclose it to you."

B. As Explained by Paul

1. 1 Corinthians 12:3

   Paul said, "I make known to you, that no one speaking by the Spirit of God says, 'Jesus is accursed.'" Apparently some of the Corinthians had called Jesus accursed while speaking in an ecstatic language that they thought had been prompted by the Holy Spirit. But the Spirit would never do that. Such practices reflected the spiritual abuses taking place in the Corinthian church at that time.

   Paul continued, "No one can say, 'Jesus is Lord,' except by the Holy Spirit" (v. 3). Just as God alone grants faith and repentance, He also grants the ability to confess Jesus as Lord, which He does through His Spirit.

   The Spirit exalts and affirms the lordship of Christ for two reasons: (1) He enables believers to see Christ's glory, majesty, and authority so they might submit to His will; (2) He enables believers to see Christ's purity and righteousness so they will pattern their lives after His.

Is Christ Precious to You?

The Holy Spirit glorifies Christ to believers. In a practical sense that means Christ becomes increasingly significant and precious to us as we walk by the Spirit and are controlled by Him. Conversely, if we're walking in the flesh, we will short-circuit the Spirit's ministry and Christ will seem less precious to us. Just how precious Christ is to you is an indication of where you are spiritually.

2. 2 Corinthians 3:18

Exodus 34:29 tells us that the face of Moses shone after he met with God on Mount Sinai. God had allowed Moses to see a portion of His glory (Ex. 33:18-23), and somehow His glory radiated from Moses' face.

Paul drew an analogy from the experience of Moses and said in effect that anyone who gazes at the glory of Christ will become like Him and radiate His glory. The more of Christ you see, the more like Him you become. That's the gist of 2 Corinthians 3:18: "We all, with unveiled face beholding as in a mirror the glory of the Lord, are being transformed into the same image from glory to glory, just as from the Lord, the Spirit."

As we gaze at Christ in God's Word, we go from one level of glory to the next—we become more like Him, and that is the Spirit's work. The literal Greek text reads, "It's being done from the Lord the Spirit."

The Holy Spirit glorifies Christ by placing His glory on display through the Word and by transforming believers into His image. The more we meditate on Christ's beauty and majesty, the more we become like Him.

Paul longed to see Christ's glory reflected in every believer. He told the Galatians, "I am . . . in labor until Christ is formed in you" (Gal. 4:19). But for Christ to be formed in them, they had to forsake their attempts to be sanctified by human efforts and return to depending on the Holy Spirit. It's the same for us.

We can't become like Christ through human efforts or apart from the Spirit.

IV. THE HOLY SPIRIT GUIDES BELIEVERS

In addition to revealing God's truth in Scripture (2 Tim. 3:16), the Spirit guides believers into God's will. That principle is taught throughout Scripture.

A. As Explained by Ezekiel

Ezekiel 36:27 says, "I will put My Spirit within you and cause you to walk in My statutes, and you will be careful to observe My ordinances." That's a promise of the New Covenant, which includes all believers. If revealing and illuminating God's truth were the extent of the Spirit's ministry, why would we need Him in us? But the Spirit also applies Scripture to our lives, thereby transforming us and producing obedience to God's will.

B. As Explained by David

1. Psalm 143:10

   David prayed, "Teach me to do Thy will, for Thou art my God." Is that your prayer also?

2. Psalm 119:35-36, 133

   David also prayed, "Make me walk in the path of Thy commandments, for I delight in it. Incline my heart to Thy testimonies. . . . Establish my footsteps in Thy word, and do not let any iniquity have dominion over me."

3. Psalm 51:6

   David said, "Thou [God] dost desire truth in the innermost being. And in the hidden part Thou wilt make me know wisdom." He knew God would show him His will in his inner being.

C. As Explained by Luke

1. Acts 13:2

When the leaders of the church at Antioch were decid-
ing whom to send as missionaries, the Holy Spirit said
to them, "Set apart for Me Barnabas and Saul for the
work to which I have called them." That was a special
revelatory act of the Spirit, but it illustrates His role in
guiding the first-century church leaders into God's will.

2. Acts 15:28

After considering the issue of how much Jewish law
should be imposed on Gentile Christians, the Jerusalem
Council drafted a letter explaining their decision. It said
in part, "It seemed good to the Holy Spirit and to us to
lay upon you no greater burden than these essentials."
They had arrived at a consensus that reflected God's
will. How did they know that? Because the Holy Spirit
had led them subjectively and had given them that
assurance.

D. As Explained by Paul

1. Romans 8:14

Paul said, "All who are being led by the Spirit of God,
these are sons of God." All true believers are led by the
Spirit.

2. Romans 9:1

Paul said, "I am telling the truth in Christ, I am not
lying, my conscience bearing me witness in the Holy
Spirit." One way the Spirit guides us is through our
conscience.

Do You Have Seemingly Unsolvable Problems?

Many people today are paralyzed with fear and anxiety. They can't
solve their own problems, and they don't know what to do or

where to go for help. Perhaps they've turned to the wrong sources for help and found them empty. Sadly, some of those people are Christians. But that shouldn't be. God has not withdrawn His Spirit from us. He's available. And through Him we have access to every resource we need.

Unbelievers must turn to Christ, who will graciously redeem them by the power of His Spirit. Believers must learn to depend on the Spirit's ministry to sustain them and guide them into God's will. We won't find solutions to our problems in human resources alone.

E. As Explained by A. W. Pink

Theologian A. W. Pink wrote about the subjective leading of the Holy Spirit, saying that those who are directed by Him are moved to examine their hearts and take frequent notice of their ways, mourn over their carnality, confess their sins, and earnestly seek grace to enable them to be obedient (*The Holy Spirit* [Grand Rapids: Baker, 1970], cf. pp. 110-15). To determine if you're being led by the Spirit, ask yourself if you examine your motives and actions. Do you correct your behavior when you're out of line with God's standards? Do you mourn over your sin and eagerly confess it to God? Do you earnestly seek God's grace so that you can obey Him? If so, you're walking in the Spirit. And by doing so, you will know God's will.

Conclusion

The Spirit is both the source and sustainer of our spiritual life, which began with His work of conviction, repentance, and regeneration. He then indwelt, baptized, gifted, secured, and separated us from sin and death. That's what it means to begin in the Spirit (Gal. 3:3). And what was begun by the Spirit cannot be perfected by human efforts apart from His power.

As we continue in the Spirit, He provides access to God, illumination of God's Word, an understanding of Christ's glory, and guidance into God's will. What a wonderful, gracious, and sufficient God we have!

46

Focusing on the Facts

1. What point does Joseph Carroll's experience in Asheville, North Carolina, illustrate (see pp. 37-38)?
2. God provides everything we need for _____ and _____ (see p. 38).
3. Psalm 23 illustrates the _____ of God's provision to believers (see p. 38).
4. What was Paul's view of God's sufficiency for meeting believers' needs (Phil. 4:19; see p. 39)?
5. How did St. Augustine express his love for Christ (see p. 40)?
6. What helped Hudson Taylor deal with the loss of his first wife (see pp. 40-41)?
7. Identify two ways in which the Holy Spirit glorifies Christ (see p. 41).
8. How does the Holy Spirit bear witness of Christ (John 15:26; see p. 42)?
9. What are two reasons the Holy Spirit exalts and affirms the lordship of Christ (see p. 42)?
10. What is one practical result of the Spirit's glorifying Christ (see p. 43)?
11. What analogy does Paul use in 2 Corinthians 3:18 to illustrate the transforming work of the Spirit within a believer (see p. 43)?
12. What promise is given in Ezekiel 36:27 (see p. 44)?
13. Are all Christians led by the Holy Spirit? Explain (Rom. 8:14; see p. 45).
14. According to A. W. Pink, how can we know if we are being led by God's Spirit (see p. 46)?

Pondering the Principles

1. Joseph Carroll's experience (see pp. 37-38) is a good illustration of how we attempt to accomplish God's work by human means, apart from divine resources. Unfortunately, that's a common problem among Christians. Perhaps you are attempting to solve a problem apart from the Spirit's power. Remember, God has made provision for every human need, and His Spirit is the key to gaining access to those provisions. Read Matthew 6:25-34 and Philippians 4:6-9. What specific promises does God make in

those passages? What does He require of you? Are you willing to do your part?

2. As the Holy Spirit glorifies Christ in our lives, Christ becomes increasingly significant and precious to us. One way to glorify Christ is to rehearse His characteristics and works. Select one of the following characteristics each day for one week. Meditate on that attribute and its implications in your life. Spend time in prayer thanking Christ for His immeasurable glory and grace.

    • His deity—Hebrews 1:8
    • His creative power—Colossians 1:16
    • His sinlessness—Hebrews 4:15-16
    • His changelessness—Hebrews 13:8
    • His sacrificial love—Romans 5:8
    • His compassion—Matthew 9:36
    • His humility—Philippians 2:5-7

4

The Ministries of the Holy Spirit—Part 3

Outline

Introduction

Review
I. The Holy Spirit Provides Access to God
II. The Holy Spirit Illuminates Scripture
III. The Holy Spirit Glorifies Christ
IV. The Holy Spirit Guides Believers

Lesson
V. The Holy Spirit Ministers Through Believers
  A. The Need for Mutual Ministries
    1. The potential sufficiency of believers
    2. The practical inadequacy of believers
  B. The Manifestation of Mutual Ministries
    1. Associating with other believers
    2. Using your spiritual gifts
      a) The definition of spiritual gifts
      b) The analogy of spiritual gifts
      c) The diversity of spiritual gifts
      d) The purpose of spiritual gifts
      e) The conduit for spiritual gifts
    3. Fulfilling the "one anothers" of Scripture
      a) The principle explained
      b) The principle illustrated
VI. The Holy Spirit Strengthens Believers
  A. To Accomplish Great Things
    1. The scope of His power
    2. An illustration of His power
  B. To Win at Spiritual Warfare
  C. To Cope with Burdens

49

Introduction

Despite the sufficiency of the spiritual resources available to believers through the Holy Spirit, many Christians attempt to reach spiritual maturity apart from the His power. They unwittingly substitute psychology and pragmatism for true spirituality. Additionally, the controversy brought about by the charismatic movement has made many Christians reluctant to speak definitively about the Spirit's ministry for fear of offending those who disagree.

Pastors who teach the sufficiency of the Spirit to meet our needs and solve our problems have been accused of being unsophisticated and of misunderstanding modern psychological principles. And believers who take the Holy Spirit seriously are often thought of as esoteric and mystical, living on an unrealistic, spiritual plane.

Each of those factors has contributed to the problem of attempting to perfect in the flesh what was begun in the Spirit (Gal. 3:3). But the fact is, only the Spirit can finish and perfect what He began in the first place. All attempts to reach spiritual maturity through human means lack divine power and therefore produce weak Christians. That in turn weakens the church. Paul told the Corinthians, "I, brethren, could not speak to you as to spiritual men, but as to men of flesh, as to babes in Christ" (1 Cor. 3:1). Correcting such a problem is difficult because fleshly Christians tend to resist spiritual counsel. Nevertheless, we must continue to call Christians back to living on the spiritual plane.

Review

We have seen that the Christian life begins in the power of the Spirit (see pp. 23-26). It is a supernatural work that ushers you into life on a spiritual level. You have been translated out of the kingdom of darkness into the kingdom of God's dear Son (Col. 1:13). You have been lifted out of the earthly realm into the heavenlies (Eph. 2:6). You function on a spiritual plane, but you can't grow on that plane if you're living in the flesh. The Spirit must continue to perfect the work He started when He saved you.

In addition to His initial work of salvation, the Spirit performs the ongoing work of sanctification:

I. THE HOLY SPIRIT PROVIDES ACCESS TO GOD (see pp. 26-29)

II. THE HOLY SPIRIT ILLUMINATES SCRIPTURE (see pp. 30-31)

III. THE HOLY SPIRIT GLORIFIES CHRIST (see pp. 41-44)

IV. THE HOLY SPIRIT GUIDES BELIEVERS (see pp. 44-46)

Those are tremendous resources that are available only through the Spirit. But that's not all He does.

Lesson

V. THE HOLY SPIRIT MINISTERS THROUGH BELIEVERS

A. The Need for Mutual Ministries

1. The potential sufficiency of believers

When we consider the resources that believers have through the Holy Spirit, we might conclude that a Christian has everything he needs to live a godly life —even without the support of other believers. In a sense that's true. Each believer is potentially sufficient because he or she is indwelt by the Holy Spirit, who is Himself sufficient.

2. The practical inadequacy of believers

Even though the Spirit is sufficient, sin prevents believers from fully appropriating their divine resources. Therefore, God uses believers to stimulate one another toward using the resources available to them through the Spirit.

B. The Manifestation of Mutual Ministries

There are several ways by which Christians can minister to one another.

1. Associating with other believers

It is obvious that we must associate with other Christians before we can minister to them. Hebrews 10:23 says, "Let us hold fast the confession of our hope without wavering, for He who promised is faithful." That is a call to consistency and faithfulness in our spiritual lives, and we become consistent by considering "how to stimulate one another to love and good deeds, not forsaking our own assembling together" (vv. 24-25).

Our goal in associating with other believers is to stimulate one another toward spiritual progress.

2. Using your spiritual gifts

We help one another grow spiritually by exercising our spiritual gifts within the context of righteous relationships. Thus we build the foundation for mutual encouragement and accountability.

a) The definition of spiritual gifts

A spiritual gift is a channel through which the Holy Spirit ministers to the Body of Christ. It's a "manifestation of the Spirit for the common good" (1 Cor. 12:7).

When believers gather together they should do so to worship God and exercise their spiritual gifts in stimulating one another to love and good deeds (Heb. 10:24). That is true Christian fellowship.

b) The analogy of spiritual gifts

Paul said, "Just as we have many members in one body and all the members do not have the same function, so we, who are many, are one body in Christ, and individually members one of another" (Rom. 12:4-5). That's a simple analogy of a body and its various members. Each member performs a different function, but each function is crucial for the overall health and effectiveness of the body.

The church is the Body of Christ (v. 5), and its members (individual believers) function so that we serve one another.

c) The diversity of spiritual gifts

Verses 6-8 say, "Since we have gifts that differ according to the grace given to us, let each exercise them accordingly: if prophecy, according to the proportion of his faith; if service, in his serving; or he who teaches, in his teaching; or he who exhorts, in his exhortation; he who gives, with liberality; he who leads, with diligence; he who shows mercy, with cheerfulness." Those are different categories of spiritual gifts.

First Corinthians 12:4 says, "There are varieties of gifts, but the same Spirit." There is only one Holy Spirit, but He distributes a variety of gifts to believers.

d) The purpose of spiritual gifts

Verses 7 and 11 say, "To each one is given the manifestation of the Spirit for the common good. . . . But one and the same Spirit works all these things, distributing to each one individually just as He wills."

The Holy Spirit empowers us to minister to one another through our spiritual gifts. One day my son Mark said to me, "Dad, when you preach you're really something special, but at home you're nothing special at all." He meant it as a compliment, and I took it that way. He recognized that something happens to me when I minister in the power of a Spirit-given gift. That's how it is with all spiritual gifts.

Are You Listening to the Holy Spirit?

One of the ways the Holy Spirit speaks to us is through the ministry of other believers. Do you receive their ministry in that way? For example, when someone encourages you toward greater faithfulness in the study of God's Word, prayer, church attendance, or ministry, do you recognize the Spirit's voice in them; or do you see it as merely another's opinion?

One of the great riches of being in full-time ministry and spending each day with the members of our church staff is the constant stimulation and accountability they bring to my life. That stimulation may come by way of exhortation, instruction, or encouragement, but I see it as God's Spirit ministering to me through them. To be in that kind of environment is a wonderful gift from God to those who bear great spiritual responsibility and need a high level of stimulation and accountability.

Even if you are not in a pastoral ministry, you still need to recognize the Spirit's ministry through other believers. Remember, a true stimulator (Heb. 10:24) speaks on behalf of the Spirit. Are you listening to what He says to you through fellow believers?

e) The conduit for spiritual gifts

All spiritual gifts must be channeled through the conduit of love.

(1) Romans 5:5—"The love of God has been poured out within our hearts through the Holy Spirit who was given to us." There is an inextricable link between God's Spirit and God's love. When we received His Spirit, we received His love as

well. We must therefore exercise our spiritual gifts in love.

(2) Romans 15:30—"I urge you, brethren, by our Lord Jesus Christ and by the love of the Spirit." Again we see a connection between the Spirit and love.

(3) Colossians 1:8—Paul commended the Colossian believers for their "love in the Spirit."

(4) Ephesians 4:15—We are always to "[speak] the truth in love."

3. Fulfilling the "one anothers" of Scripture

   a) The principle explained

   The Spirit also ministers through the "one anothers" of the New Testament: we're to love one another, pray for one another, edify one another, comfort one another, exhort one another, rebuke one another, teach one another, and many more. Those are our spiritual responsibilities toward other believers.

   b) The principle illustrated

   In Galatians 6:1-2 we have an example of mutual ministry within the church: "Brethren, even if a man is caught in any trespass, you who are spiritual, restore such a one in a spirit of gentleness; each one looking to yourself, lest you too be tempted. Bear one another's burdens, and thus fulfill the law of Christ." That's a reference to a Christian who has fallen into some kind of sin. The Greek word translated "caught" speaks of being trapped or in bondage. Today we would say he has an addiction.

   Paul instructed believers ("brethren") to deal with such problems. He did not say, "Find a local Greek philosopher who can help him." Spiritual Christians bear the responsibility of restoring those who are caught in a sinful addiction. In doing so we fulfill the law of Christ, which is the royal law recorded in James 2:8 (cf. John 13:34-35).

Whom Should Christians Turn to in Times of Trouble?

The Bible says nothing about professional help for Christians in turmoil, but it does say that Spirit-filled believers are to minister to such people. I think part of the reason people go outside the church for help is that many churches have failed to gently restore fallen believers and lovingly bear their burdens (Gal. 6:1-2).

When Christians fall into traps of despair, discouragement, depression, immorality, and substance abuse, the church should function as a healing community for such people. Spiritual believers have the responsibility of helping to restore them.

True biblical counseling to Christians in need is the process by which a Spirit-controlled Christian leads another believer to spirituality through prayer and studying the Word. There's no fleshly way to accomplish that; it is a spiritual ministry. In addition, I believe that although certain people are wonderfully gifted counselors, the restoration of sinning Christians is a ministry of the whole congregation rather than just one individual.

One writer drew a helpful analogy that illustrates the point. It goes something like this: "Do not let discouragement drench your spirit, or fear flood your soul. Despite the howling winds of circumstance and the undercurrents of the enemy, press on in the power of the Holy Spirit as you hold firmly to the rudder of faith. Scan your horizons for a fleet of like-minded ships—vessels who adore and serve their King, the Lord Jesus Christ. Once you find them, forsake your isolated wanderings for their protection, fellowship, and instruction:

- The old ships will teach you reverence.
- Battered vessels are a practical lesson in compassion.
- Fast clippers, leading the fleet under Christ, instill obedience.
- Slow barges instruct you in patience and kindness, for they often bear the heaviest burdens.
- Front-line battleships evoke respect and humility.

- A broken boat will enlarge your heart for meeting needs.
- And even a collision with another freighter will alert each member to stay on course and faithfully follow love."

No one person—be he pastor or counselor—can teach all that. But when the church functions in the power of the Holy Spirit, all those ministries take place. That dynamic stimulates each believer toward spiritual growth.

One of the tragedies of our day is that many Christians drift away from depending on the Spirit because they get in the habit of depending on their own strength. When they finally discover their own inadequacies, they turn to the world for solutions rather than seeking God's provisions through the Spirit and through fellow believers. Whom do you turn to in times of trouble?

Because the Spirit ministers to us through other believers, we must never cut ourselves off from that vital source of stimulation and accountability. Unfortunately, some Christians can attend church or Bible study week after week and make little or no contribution to the lives of other believers—and receive little or nothing from them. Others spend time with Christians, but the topic of conversation is seldom of any spiritual significance. Be sure to make the most of the Spirit's ministry through other believers!

VI. THE HOLY SPIRIT STRENGTHENS BELIEVERS

Just as a battery-operated toy needs power to run properly, Christians need supernatural power to function on the spiritual plane. Even though the Spirit gives us access to God, illuminates His Word, glorifies Christ, guides us, and ministers through us, our ability to trust Him to accomplish those things in our lives is limited by sin. Therefore, He also gives us the strength to live a victorious, joyful, and productive Christian life.

The Bible mentions several specific things for which the Spirit gives believers strength:

A. To Accomplish Great Things

1. The scope of His power

Paul said, "I bow my knees before the Father, from whom every family in heaven and on earth derives its name, that He would grant you, according to the riches of His glory, to be strengthened with power through His Spirit in the inner man" (Eph. 3:14-16). Paul prayed that his readers would be strengthened in equal measure to the riches of God's glory. Since God is infinitely rich in glory, Paul was asking for infinite spiritual strength for believers.

The scope of God's power is illustrated in verse 20: "Now to Him who is able to do exceeding abundantly beyond all that we ask or think, according to the power that works within us." That's an unimaginable, incalculable amount of power, yet it's available to every believer through the indwelling Holy Spirit. What a tremendous reality!

2. An illustration of His power

Paul had firsthand knowledge of God's power because he lived a very difficult, lonely life and depended on the Spirit's power to fight the many physical and spiritual battles he faced. His personal testimony was: "We are hard-pressed on all sides, but we are never frustrated; we are puzzled, but never in despair. We are persecuted, but are never deserted: we may be knocked down but we are never knocked out! Every day we experience something of the death of Jesus, so that we may also show the power of the life of Jesus in these bodies of ours. . . . We are always facing physical death, so that you may know spiritual life. . . . This is the reason why we never lose heart. The outward man does indeed suffer wear and tear, but every day the inward man receives fresh strength" (2 Cor. 4:8-10, 12, 16, Phillips*).

* *New Testament in Modern English.*

No matter what trials we face, the Spirit provides fresh strength each day. That's important because any level of ministry can be painful, discouraging, and heart-breaking at times. On the outside you can be getting quite a bruising, but if you live on the spiritual level there is a constant supply of fresh strength. That is the ministry of the Spirit.

B. To Win at Spiritual Warfare

The Spirit also gives us strength to fight against Satan and his forces. Paul said, "Though we walk in the flesh, we do not war according to the flesh, for the weapons of our warfare are not of the flesh, but divinely powerful for the destruction of fortresses" (2 Cor. 10:3-4).

We are human, but we can't fight spiritual battles with fleshly weapons. Therefore God has given us spiritual weapons such as prayer, His Word, and His wisdom. Such weapons are so powerful that they can destroy every spiritual fortress that Satan attempts to build in this world through satanic ideas, ideals, and values. Paul said, "We are destroying speculations and every lofty thing raised up against the knowledge of God, and we are taking every thought captive to the obedience of Christ" (v. 5). By the Spirit's power we can win every spiritual battle.

C. To Cope with Burdens

The French Reformer John Calvin noted that the Spirit lifts us up as He places Himself under our heavy burdens. Jesus referred to the Holy Spirit as the Comforter (John 14:16), One who helps carry our burdens (2 Cor. 13:14).

D. To Overcome Sin

In Galatians 5:16 Paul says, "Walk by the Spirit, and you will not carry out the desire of the flesh."

E. To Evangelize the Lost

Jesus said, "You shall receive power when the Holy Spirit has come upon you; and you shall be My witnesses" (Acts 1:8).

F. To Maintain Hope

The Spirit gives us the assurance of our eternal hope. Paul prayed, "May the God of hope fill you with all joy and peace in believing, that you may abound in hope by the power of the Holy Spirit" (Rom. 15:13).

G. To Serve God

Ephesians 3:20 says, "[God] is able to do exceeding abundantly beyond all that we ask or think, according to the power that works within us."

H. To Praise God

Ephesians 5:18-19 says, "Be filled with the Spirit, speaking to one another in psalms and hymns and spiritual songs, singing and making melody with your heart to the Lord."

I. To Establish Proper Relationships

In Ephesians 5:22–6:9 Paul gives a list of interpersonal relationships that flow from Spirit-filled lives. Included are wives who submit to their husbands, husbands who love their wives, children who obey their parents, parents who don't exasperate their children, employees who serve their employers with respect and integrity, and employers who are gracious to their employees.

Those are all ways that the Spirit strengthens believers. There are no human means by which those things can be accomplished. For example, there's no technique for overcoming sin and there's no method of evangelism that is effective apart from the Spirit's power.

VII. THE HOLY SPIRIT INTERCEDES FOR BELIEVERS

Even with all the resources of the Spirit at our disposal, we can fail Him by falling into sin. During such times He does not forsake us but ministers to us through intercessory prayer.

A. The Purpose of His Intercession (Rom. 8:26a)

"The Spirit also helps our weakness; for we do not know how to pray as we should."

The context of Romans 8 is the day when we will see Christ and when all creation will be set free from the bondage of sin (v. 21). It's the culmination of our salvation. The Greek word translated "weakness" in Romans 8:26 speaks of our inability to keep ourselves saved. Our weakness extends to the point that we don't even know how to pray effectively for ourselves. In fact, if we had to depend on our own prayers to keep us saved, we'd be lost. But when God saved us He promised to secure our salvation for eternity. We can trust His promise because He has the power to fulfill it. God exercises His power to accomplish His promises. We are eternally secure because the Holy Spirit is working in us to effect salvation.

B. The Process of His Intercession (Rom. 8:26b-27)

"The Spirit Himself intercedes for us with groanings too deep for words; and He who searches the hearts knows what the mind of the Spirit is, because He intercedes for the saints according to the will of God."

From within us the Holy Spirit is constantly interceding to the throne of God on our behalf with utterances too profound to put into words. Because He is in perfect communion with the Father and understands the Father's will perfectly, the Spirit can pray perfectly about our needs.

C. The Product of His Intercession (Rom. 8:28-39)

"We know that God causes all things to work together for good to those who love God, to those who are called according to His purpose" (v. 28).

The result of the Spirit's intercessory ministry is the ultimate working together of all things for the believer's future glory. Therefore you will one day be fully glorified and conformed to the image of Christ (vv. 28-30). It is guaranteed! Nothing can thwart God's purpose or separate you from His love (vv. 31-39).

Despite our sins, failures, inability to pray as we should, and all the obstacles we face on the human level, the Spirit continues His intercessory ministry. In addition, Jesus Himself "always lives to make intercession for [us]" (Heb. 7:25). Is it any wonder that all things are working together for our eternal good?

The Believer's Assurance of Victory

The Spirit's intercessory ministry is the guarantee of our spiritual victory. We cannot ultimately fail because He prays for us, and God answers His prayers and strengthens us. The Holy Spirit sees sin in our lives and prays to the Father to cleanse us as He brings it to our attention and leads us to repent of it. The Father then forgives us, and the Spirit empowers us each day to live more godly lives.

However, that marvelous reality doesn't relieve us of our responsibility to walk by the Spirit (Gal. 5:16) and be filled with the Spirit (Eph. 5:18).

Conclusion

The Holy Spirit is sufficient for all our needs, but many Christians turn to fleshly solutions for spiritual problems rather than drawing on their divine resources. Remember, you cannot perfect in the flesh what was begun in the Spirit (Gal. 3:3). Therefore, draw daily upon the power of the Spirit through fervent prayer and the study of God's Word.

Focusing on the Facts

1. All attempts to reach spiritual maturity through human means lack divine power and therefore produce _____ Christians (see p. 50).

2. Even though the Spirit is sufficient, _____ prevents believers from fully appropriating their divine resources (see p. 52).
3. Identify three ways that Christians minister to one another (see pp. 52-56).
4. Why is it important for a Christian to associate with other believers (Heb. 10:24-25; see p. 52)?
5. What is a spiritual gift (1 Cor. 12:7; see pp. 52-53)?
6. What analogy did Paul use to describe the function of spiritual gifts (Rom. 12:4-5; see p. 53)?
7. Is there more than one spiritual gift? Explain (Rom. 12:6-8; 1 Cor. 12:4; see p. 53).
8. One of the ways the Holy Spirit speaks to us is through the ministry of _____ _____ (see p. 54).
9. What is the conduit for spiritual gifts (see pp. 54-55)?
10. _____ _____ bear the responsibility of restoring those who are caught in a sinful addiction (see p. 55).
11. Define biblical counseling (see p. 56).
12. What was Paul's prayer request in Ephesians 3:14-16 (see p. 58)?
13. Identify three spiritual weapons God has given to every believer (see p. 59).
14. How does the Holy Spirit help believers cope with their burdens (see p. 59)?
15. According to Ephesians 3:20, what is God able to accomplish through believers (see p. 60)?
16. Why is it necessary for the Holy Spirit to intercede on behalf of believers (Rom. 8:26; see p. 61)?
17. How does the Holy Spirit intercede for believers (Rom. 8:26-27; see p. 61)?
18. What is the result of the Spirit's intercessory ministry (Rom. 8:28-39; see pp. 61-62)?
19. How does the Spirit's intercessory ministry guarantee the believer's ultimate spiritual victory (see p. 62)?

Pondering the Principles

1. We have seen that the Holy Spirit equips every believer to minister to the Body of Christ (1 Cor. 12:7, 11). Our spiritual gifts may differ, but each of us has an important contribution to make to the overall spiritual health and effectiveness of the church.

Are you a good steward of your spiritual gifts? Remember, other believers are counting on you!

2. Many Christians want to accomplish great things for God, but they become discouraged by feelings of inadequacy. The truth is that in ourselves none of us is adequate for spiritual service. But God is "able to do exceeding abundantly beyond all that we ask or think, according to the power that works within us" (Eph. 3:20). Moses is a biblical example of someone who needed to learn that lesson. Read the account of his calling in Exodus 3:1–4:30. What did God want to accomplish through Moses (Ex. 3:10)? How did Moses express his feelings of inadequacy (Ex. 3:11, 13; 4:1, 10, 13)? How did God assure him that he would not fail (Ex. 3:12, 14-23; 4:2-9, 11-12, 14-17)? Did Moses succeed at what God called him to do (Ex. 4:29-31; 12:29-36, 51)? What are you trusting God to accomplish through you today? Have you committed it to Him in prayer?

5
Walking by the Spirit

Outline

Introduction
A. Spiritual Folly
   1. Israel Forsook the True God
   2. Israel Sought a False Substitute
B. Spiritual Wisdom
   1. The spiritual issue
   2. The Spirit's initiative

Review

Lesson
 I. The Command (v. 16)
   A. The Problem
   B. The Meaning
   C. The Application
      1. What to do
      2. Why to do it
      3. How to do it
      4. The result
II. The Conflict (vv. 17-18)
   A. Explaining the Problem
   B. Defining the Flesh
      1. The body
      2. Human effort
      3. The unredeemed nature
   C. Dealing with the Flesh
   D. Compounding the Problem
      1. The mistake examined
      2. The mistake illustrated
      3. The mistake exposed

III. The Contrast (vv. 19-23)
   A. The Deeds of the Flesh (vv. 19-21)
   B. The Fruit of the Spirit (vv. 22-23)
      1. Its meaning
      2. Its power
      3. Its simplicity
IV. The Conquest (vv. 24-25)
   A. God's Part (v. 24)
   B. Our Part (v. 25)
      1. Biblically delineated
      2. Experientially applied
         a) Toward your marriage
         b) Toward yourself
         c) Toward your family

Conclusion

Introduction

In Galatians 3:3 Paul writes: "Are you so foolish? Having begun by the Spirit, are you now being perfected by the flesh?"

A. Spiritual Folly

We are as foolish as the Galatians when we begin our salvation in the Spirit and then try to live in the flesh. Yet it is an old error. Jeremiah 2:11-13 is God's indictment of Israel when they similarly defected spiritually: " 'Has a nation changed gods when they were not gods? But My people have changed their glory for that which does not profit. Be appalled, O heavens, at this, and shudder, be very desolate,' declares the Lord. 'For My people have committed two evils: they have forsaken Me, the fountain of living waters, to hew for themselves cisterns, broken cisterns, that can hold no water.' "

1. Israel forsook the true God

Israel forsook the true God, the source of everything. In John 7:37-38 Jesus says, "If any man is thirsty, let him come to Me and drink. He who believes in Me, as the

Scripture said, 'From his innermost being shall flow rivers of living water.' " He was referring to the ministry of the Holy Spirit, the divine resource who provides all that a thirsty soul needs. Just as Israel forsook God, the "fountain of living waters" (Jer. 2:13), the church today has forsaken God the Holy Spirit, who remains the provision of all we need.

2. Israel sought a false substitute

Israel turned from God to substitutes that could not help. They turned to broken cisterns that held no water —which promised everything yet provided nothing. The church commits the same folly today when it turns from the Holy Spirit—the stream of living water—and seeks answers in the empty buckets of psychology, pragmatism, and humanism.

B. Spiritual Wisdom

1. The spiritual issue

Salvation is a supernatural work of the Holy Spirit. The believer's spiritual life is also His supernatural work. The Galatian sin was believing that what was begun in the Spirit could be perfected in the flesh.

2. The Spirit's initiative

As Christians we came into spiritual life through the agency of the Holy Spirit. The Holy Spirit convicted us of our sin and brought us to repentance. He produced in us the faith we needed to respond to the preaching of the gospel. He similarly brought us into submission to the lordship of Christ, and we were regenerated by Him—recreated into new life. The Spirit of God indwelt us, baptized us into the Body of Christ, gave us spiritual gifts, sealed us for eternal life, and separated us from sin. That monumental work of the Spirit lifted us out of the kingdom of darkness into the kingdom of God's dear Son (Col. 1:13). Ours is a spiritual life—we are not of this world, though we are in this world.

Review

We have previously seen that the Spirit offers believers all the perfecting resources they need. He provides access to God, where all spiritual resources are found (see pp. 26-29). He illuminates the Scriptures so that believers may know exactly what they are called to do (see pp. 30-31). He strengthens believers in the inner man and glorifies Christ as the authority and example of Christian practice (see pp. 40-41). He personally guides the consciences of believers to do God's will (see pp. 44-46). He ministers strength and correction to believers through other believers, and intercedes for us so that all things work together for good in our lives (see pp. 51-62). Those are the ministries that the Spirit of God offers every Christian to bring about spiritual maturity.

We are to live on the spiritual level. Therefore, we must cease doing what we are warned against in Scripture.

A. 1 Thessalonians 5:19—"Do not quench the Spirit." We quench the Spirit when we seek solutions apart from His leading. We put out His fire in our lives, push Him aside, and treat Him with indifference when we deny His power.

B. Ephesians 4:30—"Do not grieve the Holy Spirit of God." The church today is both quenching and grieving the Spirit by refusing to respond to His leading and by engaging in sin and disobedience. We must begin to move in the power of the Spirit if the church is ever to stop offering human solutions to spiritual problems.

Lesson

In Galatians 5 Paul tells us that the key to Christian living is a Spirit-controlled life. Our problem is our fallen flesh, and only the Holy Spirit can harness it. Every wrong action, reaction, word, idea, emotion, and attitude is from the flesh. The Bible says salvation changed our inner man (Rom. 8:10). Some day we'll be changed in the outer man and will be perfect forever. When our bodies have been redeemed, the flesh will no longer be a problem.

I. THE COMMAND (v. 16)

"Walk by the Spirit, and you will not carry out the desire of the flesh."

A. The Problem

Christians are clearly commanded to subdue the flesh. Subjection of the flesh is the foundation of the Christian life. When a Christian is walking in the Spirit, the desires of the flesh are not carried out. Since all our sin problems are caused by the flesh, the means by which the flesh is overcome is the solution to everything. That is not an over-simplification but the truth according to God's Word.

B. The Meaning

The Greek word translated "walk" is a present tense command. It could be translated "keep on continually walking." Paul used a picturesque metaphor to describe the Christian life—we're to take one step at a time under the control of the Holy Spirit. The Christian walk is a habitual pattern.

As Christians we possess the indwelling Spirit (Rom. 8:9). In fact our bodies are the temple of the Holy Spirit (1 Cor. 6:19). As the Spirit moves and leads, we are to respond moment by moment, step by step, and day by day, relying on His power and direction.

C. The Application

1. What to do

   Walking in the Spirit requires two things: studying the Word of God so that you can know the mind of the Spirit, and communing with God so that you can know the will of the Spirit.

   a) Ephesians 5:18-20—"Be filled with the Spirit . . . singing and making melody with your heart to the Lord; always giving thanks for all things in the name of our Lord Jesus Christ to God, even the Father."

b) Colossians 3:16—"Let the word of Christ richly dwell within you." Being filled with the Spirit is the same as letting the Word dwell in you richly, for as the Word dominates your thinking, it dominates your actions. As the Word moves through your heart and mind, the Spirit of God directs your life.

As you spend time in the Word and in prayer, communing with the living God and building an intimate relationship with Him, you will be in a position for the Spirit to move you down the path of God's choosing.

2. Why to do it

The Bible does not teach the eradication of sin in this life or a second work of grace whereby a person becomes perfect and never sins again. The spiritual walk is accomplished moment by moment and depends on our submissiveness. Anyone who says he has no sin makes God a liar (1 John 1:8-10). Although we can't overcome sin totally in this life, we can overcome it as a pattern of life by walking by the Spirit. We must cultivate spiritual thinking by communing with the living God in constant and intense prayer, and by feeding continually on the Word so that our thoughts are God's thoughts. That's why Paul said, "I die daily" (1 Cor. 15:31). Every day we are to die to self and walk by the Spirit.

3. How to do it

The Christian life is a daily yielding to the Spirit of God. "Walk" is a general term that describes the Christian life.

a) Ephesians 4:1-2—"Walk in a manner worthy of the calling with which you have been called, with all humility and gentleness."

b) 1 Corinthians 7:17—"As the Lord has assigned to each one, as God has called each, in this manner let him walk."

c) 2 Corinthians 5:7—"We walk by faith, not by sight."

d) Ephesians 2:10—We were "created in Christ Jesus for good works, which God prepared beforehand, that we should walk in them."

e) Ephesians 4:17—"Walk no longer just as the Gentiles also walk, in the futility of their mind."

f) 2 Thessalonians 3:6—"Keep aloof from every brother who leads an unruly life." We are to walk apart from sin.

g) Ephesians 5:2—"Walk in love."

h) Ephesians 5:8—"Walk as children of light."

i) Ephesians 5:15-16—"Be careful how you walk, not as unwise men, but as wise, making the most of your time, because the days are evil."

j) 3 John 3-4—John wrote, "You are walking in truth. I have no greater joy than this, to hear of my children walking in the truth."

For a Christian to walk in humility, purity, contentment, faith, good works, separateness, love, light, wisdom, and truth, he or she must walk by the Spirit. Only the Spirit can produce those virtues.

4. The result

All the commands of the New Testament can be reduced to the necessity of walking by the Spirit. When you walk by the Spirit, you do not carry out the lusts or desires of the flesh. Your flesh wants to control you—your actions, thoughts, and feelings. It wants to create anger, hostility, bitterness, jealousy, envy, and strife. It wants you to fear, doubt, and hate God. It wants your life to be full of guilt, your marriage destroyed, your home wrecked, and your relationships ruined. It wants to render you useless to God. The only hope of overcoming the flesh is to walk by the Spirit. Human solutions cannot solve fundamentally spiritual problems. The use of pragmatism, human methodologies, psychology, and other human efforts to solve such problems will fail to overcome the compelling lusts of the flesh. Victorious Christian living is achieved by walking by the Spirit.

II. THE CONFLICT (vv. 17-18)

"The flesh sets its desire against the Spirit, and the Spirit against the flesh; for these are in opposition to one another, so that you may not do the things that you please. But if you are led by the Spirit, you are not under the Law."

It's easy to articulate a principle, but it can be difficult to live by it.

A. Explaining the Problem

A conflict is assumed in verse 16. Paul indicates that our flesh desires to harm us and that the only way to overcome it is to walk by the Spirit. He is more specific in verse 17: the flesh is opposed to the Holy Spirit. That's why there is conflict in the life of a Christian. It's a conflict that doesn't exist in the life of a non-Christian because he doesn't possess the Spirit. Christians are different.

1. 2 Corinthians 5:17—"If any man is in Christ, he is a new creature; the old things passed away; behold, new things have come."

2. Galatians 2:20—Paul said, "I have been crucified with Christ; and it is no longer I who live, but Christ lives in me."

We are new creations—new people. In Christ we are created for good works that God has already ordained (Eph. 2:10), yet we still sin. That's because we are a new creation incarcerated in unredeemed flesh. Until our unredeemed flesh is destroyed and we are glorified, we will always have to battle the flesh.

B. Defining the Flesh

What is the flesh? The Greek word *sarx* (often translated "flesh") is a very important term in New Testament teaching.

1. The body

   Sometimes the word *sarx* refers to the physical body. In Luke 24:39 Jesus says, "A spirit does not have flesh and bones as you see that I have." Here Jesus referred to body tissue.

2. Human effort

   Sarx is also used to refer to human effort. That is how Paul used it in Galatians 3:3: "Having begun by the Spirit, are you now being perfected by the flesh?" As we've already discussed, that is an obvious reference to man's effort to accomplish the supernatural by natural means.

3. The unredeemed nature

   The primary significance of *sarx* is its reference to our unredeemed nature. When so used, it refers to that part of a Christian that hasn't yet been redeemed (Rom. 8:23). The flesh is where sin resides in us.

   The word refers not only to sin's residence in the body, but also to its effect on the mind. Scripture refutes the philosophical dualism that says spirit is good and material things are evil. *Sarx* in this sense encompasses your material body, your feelings, your thoughts, your mind— any part of you that is tainted by sin.

   Paul illustrates that concept of *sarx* in Romans 7: "I am not practicing what I would like to do, but I am doing the very thing I hate" (v. 15). He explained that he was in that state specifically because of the sin within him (v. 17), describing its residence as "the flesh" (v. 18). In salvation, one's spirit is changed and made new. But that new man remains in an old house.

   In Galatians 5:17 Paul's message is that the flesh of a saved person is not in harmony with that person's spiritual state. The unredeemed flesh and the Holy Spirit are engaged in conflict. Verse 17 notes that that conflict is of a nature that sometimes doesn't allow you to do as you'd prefer.

You may have noticed in your own spiritual walk that sometimes you don't do what you ought to do or you do what you shouldn't do. That's the battle of the Christian—Paul describes it in Romans 7. Unbelievers do not participate in this battle because it is a war between the flesh and the indwelling Holy Spirit.

C. Dealing with the Flesh

Human solutions are the products of the flesh because the flesh affects all human effort. Psychology and pragmatism represent fleshly attempts to solve spiritual problems. Those methodologies are the products of natural effort that is independent of God. When we have spiritual problems and turn to human solutions for answers, we are attempting to snuff out fire with gasoline.

The flesh "sets its desire against the Spirit, and the Spirit against the flesh" (v. 17). The Greek word translated "desire" (*epithumia*) refers to a strong compulsive yearning. The flesh desires to conceive and bring forth sin, whereas the Holy Spirit desires to prevent sin from happening altogether.

The flesh is the beachhead where temptation lands. Evil desires move the flesh in a battle against the Holy Spirit to dominate the Christian's life. The power of the flesh is great, but the power of the Spirit is greater. When we walk by the Spirit, we will not fulfill the desires of the flesh. When we pursue fleshly solutions to problems, we feed the flesh.

D. Compounding the Problem

1. The mistake examined

In verse 16 Paul says we're to walk by the Spirit, and thereby we choose not to carry out the desires of the flesh. In verse 18 he says that when we walk by the Spirit, we're not under the law. Paul equated attempts to live by the Mosaic law with the desires of the flesh. The Mosaic law was a collection of rules by which man was to control himself. If man kept the whole law he would be perfect. Such a man would be completely controlling his flesh. But no one can keep the whole law.

In verse 18 Paul is saying that when we walk by the Spirit, we are not under the law of human effort. Human effort is connected with the flesh, whereas spiritual effort is connected with the Spirit. Operating under the law means to be operating by works—by human effort, using human solutions, agendas, wisdom, and methodologies. Those only feed the flesh. Human effort is pointless when it attempts to deal with the spiritual dimension. The law, which is good in and of itself (Rom. 7:12), is unable to control the flesh. The problem with human methods, such as psychology, is that they are of human design. They are far inferior to the design of God's law and tend to heighten the desire of the flesh.

2. The mistake illustrated

In John Bunyan's classic *The Pilgrim's Progress* there is a scene in what Bunyan called "The Interpreter's House." The parlor in the house was thick with dust. Christian, the main character of the book, saw someone come in and start to sweep the dust. But it just billowed into a cloud and choked everyone in the room. Then it fell back down to where it had been. The Interpreter explained to Christian, "This parlor is the heart of a man that was never sanctified by the sweet grace of the Gospel: The dust is his Original Sin, and inward Corruptions that have defiled the whole man. He that began to sweep . . . is the Law" ([Edinburgh: Banner of Truth, 1979 reprint], p. 26). The law can only stir up the dust of sin—it cannot cleanse anyone. Pragmatism, psychology, and other human methodologies can do no better because they are inferior to the law. The flesh requires a spiritual solution.

3. The mistake exposed

The folly of human effort is that God set an impossible standard to begin with. He wants us to look to Himself. In addition to that impossible standard, Satan is a very strong foe, and the flesh is very powerful. Man will nev-

75

er be able to keep the divine standard, overcome Satan, and dominate the flesh by human means.

Every problem in life comes from the flesh. Every solution comes from the Spirit. As Christians, the encouraging truth of 2 Corinthians 6:16 ought to be embedded in our minds: "We are the temple of the living God; just as God said, 'I will dwell in them and walk among them.' " God lives in us. He is walking with us and leads us. The Spirit of almighty God is in us. We are to follow where He leads, and that is the only way we can conquer the flesh.

III. THE CONTRAST (vv. 19-23)

A. The Deeds of the Flesh (vv. 19-21)

"The deeds of the flesh are evident, which are: immorality, impurity, sensuality, idolatry, sorcery, enmities, strife, jealousy, outbursts of anger, disputes, dissensions, factions, envying, drunkenness, carousing, and things like these. . . . Those who practice such things shall not inherit the kingdom of God."

1. Sin associated with sex

Immorality, impurity, and sensuality all relate to sexual behavior. The Greek term translated "immorality" is *porneia*, meaning "illicit sex" or "fornication." "Impurity" (Gk., *akatharsia*) means "uncleanness." It refers to pornographic thoughts that lead to pornographic activities. "Sensuality" refers to lascivious conduct—living for pleasure without restraint.

A contemporary term to describe those sins is "sexual addiction." Sexual addictions are not caused by a lack of self-esteem or poor relationships with one's mother or father. They are produced by the flesh.

2. Sin associated with religion

Verse 20 lists the category of self-effort in religion and labels it "idolatry." Idolatry is as much a work of the flesh as immorality. Idolatry is worshiping or being preoccupied with anything other than the true God—such

76

as false gods, false religious systems, self, money, career, prestige, houses, or cars.

3. Sins associated with drugs

The Greek word translated "sorcery" is *pharmakia* (meaning "drugs"), from which we get the English word *pharmacy*. Drugs were used in Paul's time in the practice of magic and sorcery. Because people regularly took drugs as a part of occultic practices, the term *pharmakia* came to be associated with sorcery and witchcraft. However, its root idea is related to drugs.

4. Sins associated with relationships

The flesh produces "enmities" (hostility), "strife" (quarreling), "jealousy" (anger toward another's good fortune), "outbursts of anger" (uncontrolled temper tantrums), "disputes," "dissensions," "factions," and "envying."

5. Sins associated with alcohol

The flesh produces "drunkenness" and "carousing," along with the wild parties and immoral activities associated with such vices.

All spiritual problems that people have in this world are produced by the flesh. Compulsive sexual behavior is a product of the flesh (v. 19). Obsession with the things of the world is a product of the flesh—it is "idolatry" (v. 20). Drug addiction is a product of the flesh (v. 20). Bitterness, hate, family conflicts, self-pity, jealousy, lack of fulfillment, temper problems, drinking problems, envy, discontent, and unhappiness are all the products of the flesh. Paul did not provide us with an exhaustive list. That's why he said, "things like these" (v. 21).

Paul warned that "those who practice such things shall not inherit the kingdom of God" (v. 21). Those who continually practice the deeds of the flesh are the unregenerate. If the things that Paul listed are the unbroken patterns of your life, then you're not a Christian.

B. The Fruit of the Spirit (vv. 22-23)

"The fruit of the Spirit is love, joy, peace, patience, kindness, goodness, faithfulness, gentleness, self-control; against such things there is no law."

1. Its meaning

Paul affirms that there is only one way to dominate the flesh: the fruit of the Spirit, as opposed to the products of the flesh. The law doesn't deal with those things because it deals only with human effort. The fruit of the Spirit is produced not by human effort but by the power of the Spirit.

2. Its power

A lack of love is a lack of the fruit of the Spirit. Depression and despair are a lack of joy, which is part of the fruit of the Spirit. Inner conflict and fear are a lack of peace, which is also part of the fruit of the Spirit. The Spirit produces patience, kindness, goodness, faithfulness, and gentleness in place of distraction. He gives self-con-trol to those who are out of control.

3. Its simplicity

The principles that Paul gave for the resolution of spiritual problems are simple. The only one who can overcome the flesh is the Spirit, so it makes sense to walk by the Spirit. But we often think we are clever enough with our human solutions, and we end up bewitched into trying to cure fleshly problems with human solutions. The result is a sick church.

IV. THE CONQUEST (vv. 24-25)

A. God's Part (v. 24)

"Those who belong to Christ Jesus have crucified the flesh with its passions and desires."

The flesh has been put to death. It is part of our past. But some of us are foolish enough to carry the corpse around.

We let its rotting decay affect our lives much more than necessary. Paul's instruction is that from a factual standpoint before God, the flesh is dead. The power of its desires is destroyed.

B. Our Part (v. 25)

"If we live by the Spirit, let us also walk by the Spirit."

1. Biblically delineated

The only source of spiritual transformation is the Holy Spirit. The only way to live spiritually is in accordance with the beginning of our spiritual life. We began in the Spirit, so we must live in the Spirit.

2. Experientially applied

a) Toward your marriage

Do you want to have a happy marriage? Walk by the Spirit. He will give you love, joy, and peace. If you are having terrible conflict in your marriage, it's not because you haven't had good counseling; it's because you're not walking by the Spirit.

b) Toward yourself

You may be experiencing personal problems such as dissatisfaction, unhappiness, and depression. One human solution is to claim that you have those problems because your parents spanked you when you were four. Although circumstances do complicate our lives, they do not cause spiritual problems. The reason you're not enjoying the fruit of the Spirit is that it is only for those who walk by the Spirit.

c) Toward your family

The flesh wars against the Spirit. I am often asked, "What is the key to raising your kids to love the Lord? What is the key to having a happy home?" The answer is simply to walk by the Spirit. He will produce His fruit.

Conclusion

Walking by the Spirit is hard to do on our own. It is a day-by-day yielding to the direction of the Spirit. That is why Galatians 6:1-2 says, "Brethren, even if a man is caught in any trespass [because he didn't walk by the Spirit], you who are spiritual [walking in the Spirit], restore such a one in a spirit of gentleness; each one looking to yourself, lest you too be tempted. Bear one another's burdens, and thus fulfill the law of Christ [the law of love]." Christians need help from each other. That's one reason the church exists. We're not to forsake assembling together, and we are to stimulate each other toward love and good deeds when we do meet (Heb. 10:25). Because all of life's problems stem from the flesh, we must help one another to walk by the Spirit.

Focusing on the Facts

1. What sin did Paul write the book of Galatians to combat? How does it relate to Israel's past (see pp. 66-67)?
2. The key to Christian living is a _____ _____ (see p. 68).
3. What is the source of our spiritual problems (see p. 68)?
4. What picturesque metaphor did Paul use to describe the pattern of the Christian life (p. 69)?
5. What two activities are essential in the life of a Christian (see p. 69)?
6. Do believers ever become sinless in this life? Why or why not (see p. 70)?
7. List some of the ways in which Scripture describes the walk of the Christian (see pp. 70-71).
8. What does the flesh desire to accomplish in the life of a believer (see p. 72)?
9. What different meanings does the Greek word *sarx* have in the New Testament (see pp. 72-74)?
10. What is wrong with trying to use psychology, pragmatism, and other humanly conceived methodologies to solve the problem of the flesh (see. p. 74)?
11. Was man ever able to solve the problem of the flesh by trying to fulfill the law? What does that imply (see pp. 74-75)?
12. What kind of a solution does the problem of the flesh require? Where does a Christian go to find that solution (see pp. 75-76)?

13. What are the deeds of the flesh (see pp. 76-77)?
14. How does one conquer the deeds of the flesh (see pp. 78-79)?

Pondering the Principles

1. The Galatians attempted to accomplish spiritual goals by methods of their own devising. The Puritan writer Abraham Wright stated, "The cause why our oppressors prevail oft against us is, because we trust too much in our own wits, and lean too much upon our own inventions; opposing subtility to subtility, one evil device to another, matching and maintaining policy by policy, and not committing our cause to God" (cited in *A Puritan Golden Treasury*, I. D. E. Thomas, ed. [Edinburgh: Banner of Truth, 1977], p. 294). Peter said that Christians were to humble themselves under God's mighty hand, knowing that He will lift us up in due time, and cast all our anxieties upon Him because He cares for us (1 Pet. 5:6-7). Yet in our pride we prefer man's diagnoses and solutions instead of the remedies God so richly supplies through the indwelling Holy Spirit. How are you going to seek the Spirit's supply and direction to meet your own need for spiritual strength?

2. Many in the church have adopted the idea that Christianity is merely a philosophical system for dealing with life. We often act as though we are ashamed of the gospel, forgetting it is "the power of God for the salvation of everyone who believes" (Rom. 1:16, NIV*). The Puritan William Bridge wrote that "faith tells a man that God is come near to him, and he is come near to God; and therefore faith certainly is the great remedy and means against all discouragements that can arise" (*A Lifting Up for the Downcast* [Edinburgh: Banner of Truth, 1979 reprint], p. 267). If you are a Christian, are there problems in your life that you're attempting to solve in your own strength? Rely on the Spirit instead. If you do not know Christ, are you now willing to give yourself to Him who promised, "Take My yoke upon you, and learn from Me, for I am gentle and humble in heart; and you shall find rest for your souls" (Matt. 11:29)?

* *New International Version.*

81

6
Helping Others Walk by the Spirit

Outline

Introduction

Lesson
I. The Problem
   A. The Reality of Sinfulness
   B. The Remedy to Sinfulness
      1. Personal implications
      2. Corporate implications
         a) In spiritual gifts
         b) In mutual support
   C. The Responsibility for Sinlessness
II. The Solution
   A. Pick Them Up (v. 1)
      1. Whom do we help?
      2. What prompts our helping?
      3. What prevents us from helping?
      4. Who may help?
      5. What procedure will help?
         a) In private
         b) In public
            (1) In the presence of witnesses
            (2) In the presence of the church
      6. What is our purpose in helping?
      7. What is our attitude when helping?
      8. What precaution should we take when helping?
   B. Hold Them Up (vv. 2-5)
      1. What to do
         a) Ease the load
         b) Fulfill the law

Introduction

All Christians experience times when they walk in the flesh and not by the Spirit. Even though we know about the Holy Spirit, His power, and biblical exhortations to walk in the Spirit, we all fail at various times. The Spirit is sufficient, but because we live in unredeemed flesh, we occasionally become fleshly. When that happens, we can expect those around us who are walking by the Spirit to respond biblically by confronting us. Likewise when we are walking by the Spirit, we have the responsibility to help restore fleshly Christians by confronting them.

The Christian life cannot be lived individually. Hebrews 10:24-25 says, "Let us consider how to stimulate one another to love and good deeds, not forsaking our own assembling together." The spiritual people within the church are to come alongside the fleshly people and lift them up.

Christians are one of two things at any one time: we are either spiritual or fleshly. We're spiritual when we obey the will and Word of God, are sensitive to the Spirit, and are moved along by the Spirit as we confess sin and allow Him to control our lives. We're fleshly when we're running our own lives in disobedience to the Lord. A person who has been a Christian for five minutes is spiritual if he's walking by the Spirit. A person who has been a Christian sixty years is fleshly if he's not obeying the Word of God or walking by the Spirit. Spiritual growth occurs only when we're walking by the Spirit.

Lesson

I. THE PROBLEM

A. The Reality of Sinfulness

Galatians 6 explains how we help one another to be spiritual. It is applicable to all Christians because all Christians sin.

1. James 3:2—"We all stumble in many ways."

2. 1 John 1:8—"If we say that we have no sin, we are deceiving ourselves, and the truth is not in us."

3. 1 John 1:10—"If we say that we have not sinned, we make Him [God] a liar, and His word is not in us."

B. The Remedy to Sinfulness

1. Personal implications

There is always a remedial ministry occurring in the Body of Christ—the spiritual calling the fleshly to live on the spiritual level. It is essential because a fleshly Christian is useless to God and can be harmful to His purposes.

a) 2 Timothy 2:20-21—"In a large house there are not only gold and silver vessels, but also vessels of wood and of earthenware, and some to honor and some to dishonor. Therefore, if a man cleanses himself from these things, he will be a vessel for honor, sanctified, useful to the Master, prepared for every good work." Christians are to be cleansed. If you're using human means to solve spiritual problems, you're functioning in the flesh and you are useless.

b) 1 Corinthians 5:6—"A little leaven leavens the whole lump of dough." If there's sin in a believer's life it has a negative impact throughout the Body of Christ. We must therefore be sensitive to both our own sin and that of others. Only in that way will the whole church be strong. We have the responsibility to walk by the Spirit ourselves so that we may stimulate that walk in others.

2. Corporate implications

The most important pursuit of the believer is personal holiness. That is true from both a personal and corporate standpoint. I can't deal with your problems unless I've dealt with mine first (cf. Matt. 7:1-5). Corporate ministry requires individual purity.

a) In spiritual gifts

We minister to each other by using our spiritual gifts, by which the Spirit of God ministers through us to the Body of Christ. If we operate on a fleshly level, the spiritual gifts given to us won't function properly.

b) In mutual support

All believers are called to pray for, comfort, encourage, exhort, love, and teach one another (Col. 3:12-16). For those qualities and attitudes to be functional in our lives, we must be drawing on spiritual resources.

C. The Responsibility for Sinlessness

We have a responsibility to deal with one another in regard to sin. It would be nice if we could walk by the Spirit by ourselves. Then we wouldn't need any encouragement, help, or reproof. But we do need one another. I remember someone's saying to me once, "I want to keep my life right before God for two reasons: so that God will use me to confront and help others who are sinning, and so that no one will be obliged to confront me." The ministry of restoration is self-purging. If a church does not engage in that kind of ministry, it is in effect removing a great motive for holy living.

1. 1 Corinthians 5:6-7—Paul said, "Do you not know that a little leaven leavens the whole lump of dough? Clean out the old leaven, that you may be a new lump, just as you are in fact unleavened." The church must cleanse itself. It cannot allow itself to tolerate sin among its people. The testimony of the church and the joy and effectiveness of its people are at stake.

2. 2 Thessalonians 3:6—"We command you, brethren, in the name of our Lord Jesus Christ, that you keep aloof from every brother who leads an unruly life and not according to the tradition which you received from us." When a believer has been confronted and still refuses to repent of his sin, we must stay away from him. Otherwise that person will have a negative effect on the entire church body.

3. 1 Timothy 5:20—Elders "who continue in sin, rebuke in the presence of all, so that the rest also may be fearful of sinning." Men in spiritual leadership have a great responsibility to maintain the purity of the church.

4. Titus 2:15—"These things speak and exhort and reprove with all authority. Let no one disregard you." Because God wants a pure people who are zealous for good deeds, the church must confront sin in whatever form it appears.

5. Titus 3:10-11—"Reject a factious man after a first and second warning, knowing that such a man is perverted and is sinning, being self-condemned."

II. THE SOLUTION

Since every Christian is either spiritual or fleshly at any particular time, it is safe to assume that a portion of the church is fleshly at any one time. Those who are walking by the Spirit are to help those who are fleshly. Otherwise the fleshly are cut off from the perfecting work of God in their lives. The responsibility of the spiritual to the fleshly does not apply to scandalous sin alone; it is a very broad responsibility.

A. Pick Them Up (v. 1)

"Brethren, even if a man is caught in any trespass, you who are spiritual, restore such a one in a spirit of gentleness; each one looking to yourself, lest you too be tempted."

Spiritual Christians have a responsibility to pick up the fleshly from their sin.

1. Whom do we help?

That responsibility is exercised within the church. The term "brethren" (v. 1) refers to Christians. The restoration Paul called for is for those within the church.

2. What prompts our helping?

Paul said that "any" trespass is to be the subject of confrontation. "Caught" (Gk., *prolambanō*) means "trapped," "bound by," or "in bondage to." "Trespass" (Gk., *paraptōma*) carries the idea of falling or stumbling into sin. So when a believer falls and is caught in sin, the spiritual are to act.

3. What prevents us from helping?

American culture can make it difficult to know what is going on in the lives of other believers. Often we don't get close enough to people to see the way they live. But when you do know that a brother or sister in Christ is caught in sin, you have to go into action. That is a mandate for the church.

We begin in and are perfected by the Spirit. However, we can easily fall to the fleshly level, and when we do, we're not always able to get back up on our own. We need other Christians to stimulate us again to love and good works. So the church must function as more than a Sunday morning meeting where we stare at the backs of people's heads. There must be an actual confrontation of lives.

4. Who may help?

Paul said that if a person is caught in any sin, "you who are spiritual, restore such a one" (v. 1). Those "who are spiritual" are people who have begun in the Spirit and are being perfected by Him. They are continually responding to the Spirit's ministry in their lives. They think spiritual thoughts, and the Word of Christ dwells in them richly. Paul didn't say they are perfect. But those who are confessing their sin faithfully, obeying the Word of God, and seeking the Spirit's leading through prayer are obligated to help restore brothers and sisters in Christ who are caught in sin. This is how Scripture describes those who are spiritual:

a) Galatians 5:25—"If we live by the Spirit, let us also walk by the Spirit."

b) Galatians 5:18—"If you are led by the Spirit, you are not under the Law."

c) Galatians 5:22-23—"The fruit of the Spirit is love, joy, peace, patience, kindness, goodness, faithfulness, gentleness, [and] self-control." You are spiritual if those qualities are evident in your life.

d) Ephesians 5:18-19—"Be filled with the Spirit, speaking to one another in psalms and hymns and spiritual songs, singing and making melody with your heart to the Lord." Spirit-filled people are characterized by joy, praise, and worship.

e) Ephesians 5:22–6:9—Spirit-filled husbands love their wives as Christ sacrificially loved the church (5:25-33). Spirit-filled wives submit themselves to their husbands (5:22-24, 33). Spirit-filled parents do not provoke their children (6:4). Spirit-filled children obey their parents (6:1-3). Spirit-filled employers are kind to those who work for them (6:9). Spirit-filled employees serve from the heart—as if their employers were Christ Himself (6:5-8).

A Spirit-filled life can be recognized. Mere emotions are not sufficient evidence of a Spirit-filled life. You know you're walking by the Spirit when you see something happening in your life. If you are walking by the Spirit, you will experience the fruit of the Spirit. If you lack love, joy, peace of heart, kindness, faithfulness to God, gentleness, and self-control in your life, then you're not walking by the Spirit.

Keep in mind that perfection is not required. A general pattern in your life will reflect the Spirit in you. Colossians 3:16 says, "Let the word of Christ richly dwell within you, with all wisdom teaching and admonishing one another with psalms and hymns and spiritual songs, singing with thankfulness in your hearts to God." Those are the characteristics of a Spirit-filled believer. If you are Spirit-filled, you love God's Word and want to apply it. You want to commune with God because the Spirit in your heart cries, "Abba! Father!" (Gal. 4:6).

How Long Does It Last?

You may find that you slip from being Spirit-filled to being fleshly very quickly. Have you ever finished praying and reading your Bible in the morning, and five minutes later you find yourself yelling at the kids? That's how quickly you can go from one state to the other. Did you ever go to a Bible study, spend three hours studying the deep things of God, and then get out in the car and argue with your husband all the way home? We slip that fast. That's how strong the flesh is.

It's tempting to focus on ourselves and not get involved with anyone else. But Paul said, "Brethren, admonish the unruly, encourage the fainthearted, help the weak, be patient with all men" (1 Thess. 5:14). In the church, the strong help the weak. It is the responsibility of the spiritual to help the fleshly.

5. What procedure will help?

The spiritual will be helping the fleshly only when they "restore such a one in a spirit of gentleness" (Gal. 6:1).

90

The verb *katartizō* ("to restore") means "to mend" or "repair." The spiritual walk of the fleshly is in disrepair, and the spiritual are called to come and help repair it.

a) In private

In Matthew 18 our Lord speaks about life in the church (He used the word "church" in verse 17). In verse 15 Jesus says that "if your brother sins, go and reprove him in private." In Galatians 6:1 Paul expressed a principle consistent with the Lord's teaching in Matthew 18. Some versions of Matthew 18:15 say, "if your brother sins *against thee*" (emphasis added), but that phrasing does not appear in some manuscripts. The Christian is to confront any sin of which he is aware. And that confrontation is to occur "in private" (Matt. 18:15).

Part of the process of confrontation is to help the fleshly person recognize sin as sin. Many times people will justify their sin by comparing themselves with others. We can be very self-justifying. Once the person acknowledges his sin, he needs to confess it to God, seeking His forgiveness and the power of the Holy Spirit to overcome future temptation.

b) In public

(1) In the presence of witnesses

Matthew 18:16 says, "If he does not listen to you, take one or two more with you, so that by the mouth of two or three witnesses every fact may be confirmed." The same process of confrontation takes place again but in the presence of witnesses. That is done so that an accurate report may be made, either of the fleshly person's continued disobedience or repentance.

(2) In the presence of the church

If the fleshly person still refuses to repent, verse 17 says to "tell it to the church." The whole church is to go to the fleshly person and confront him in a similar manner in the hope of picking him up out of his sin. "If he refuses to listen even to the church," verse 17 concludes, "let him be to you as a Gentile and a tax-gatherer." The unrepentant sinner must be put out of the church and regarded as an unbeliever, for just as a little leaven leavens a whole lump of dough, so the fleshly person will affect the entire church (1 Cor. 5:6-7; Gal. 5:9).

6. What is our purpose in helping?

The purpose of church discipline is restoration. We don't want to put the sinner out of the church but to lift him up and out of sin. Putting a fleshly person out of the church is a last resort for the sake of the purity and safety of the congregation.

7. What is our attitude when helping?

Restoration is to be accomplished "in a spirit of gentleness" (v. 1). The spiritual are not to be overbearing, ungracious, or unkind to the fleshly.

a) Galatians 5:22-23—The fruit of the Spirit is "gentleness." If you are walking by the Spirit and producing the fruit of the Spirit, you will be gentle. Paul's words in Galatians 6:1 come across as a statement rather than a command. The spiritual gently restore the fleshly because gentleness is a characteristic of their spirituality.

b) 2 Corinthians 2:7-8—Paul said, "You should . . . forgive and comfort [the repentant sinner], lest somehow such a one be overwhelmed by excessive sorrow. Wherefore I urge you to reaffirm your love for him." The spiritual approach discipline with forgiving hearts. They are ready to comfort and reaffirm their love for the fleshly. Their attitude is not abusive, but gentle, tender, kind, and patient.

c) 2 Thessalonians 3:15—"Do not regard [the sinning person] as an enemy, but admonish him as a brother." Restoration is accomplished by those who love and care.

8. What precaution should we take when helping?

Galatians 6:1 concludes, "Looking to yourself, lest you too be tempted." We are all tempted to sin. Spiritual people are very understanding because they know what it is to be tempted. Jesus was tempted as we are (Heb. 4:15), so He disciplines, chastens, reproves and restores us with an understanding heart. Since Jesus, who never fell into sin, is so understanding, certainly we who have fallen into sin can sympathize with others who have fallen as we have.

So the spiritual should never lord their godliness over the fleshly. "Looking to yourself" means that those who think they are spiritual must take a good look at their own susceptibility to sin before trying to deal with sin in others. That keeps the fleshly from attempting to straighten out the fleshly.

B. Hold Them Up (vv. 2-5)

"Bear one another's burdens, and thus fulfill the law of Christ. For if anyone thinks he is something when he is nothing, he deceives himself. But let each one examine his own work, and then he will have reason for boasting in regard to himself alone, and not in regard to another. For each one shall bear his own load" (Gal. 6:2-5).

The work of restoration is not finished by the initial confrontation. Verse 2 says, "Bear one another's burdens, and thus fulfill the law of Christ."

1. What to do

   a) Ease the load

   The Greek word *baros* ("burden") refers to an excessive, heavy, unbearable load. The Greek verb translated "bear" means "to carry with endurance" or "get under the load." The spiritual are to ease the burden of temptation to which the repentant brother or sister in Christ may be subject after deliverance from the trespass.

b) Fulfill the law

Bearing each other's burdens fulfills "the law of Christ" (v. 2). What is the law of Christ?

(1) John 13:34—Jesus said, "A new commandment I give to you, that you love one another, even as I have loved you." That is the law of Christ.

(2) James 1:25—Christ's law is the "perfect law, the law of liberty."

(3) Galatians 5:14—"The whole Law is fulfilled in one word, in the statement, 'You shall love your neighbor as yourself' " (Lev. 19:18). Christ's law is the law of love. It calls for the spiritual to lift up the fleshly and then keep them up by helping them bear their burdens.

Falling to the flesh is caused by the burden of temptation. The load can get so heavy that a Christian falls. The spiritual must help the tempted, or they may fall again and again. Every Christian has his own areas of weakness. We may be hit often with the same kind of temptation. Persistent, oppressive, heavy temptation is a burden that individual believers don't bear alone very well.

Sin Wants You Alone

Sin prefers to have you alone. The more often you are removed from Christian fellowship, the more tempted you will be. When you are among other believers—in a strong Christian family or in strong Christian friendships—you will benefit from the strength of those relationships. Accountability and the bearing of one another's burdens naturally occur in such settings. We don't do well alone. I know many Christian men who have to travel alone for days on end, and they have great battles with temptation that do not exist when they are in the fellowship of God's people. So the spiritual need to bear the burdens of others.

2. How to do it

   a) Accountability

   Bearing another's burdens presupposes establishing a relationship with that person. I try to help carry other people's burdens by meeting regularly with them or by having regular telephone conversations. Usually I ask the people I am helping to keep a list and report to me every time they fall into the particular temptation with which they are struggling. They don't like to do that because they don't want me to read that list. So they avoid the sin. Accountability will help someone carry the load of temptation.

   b) Prayer

   Faithful prayer is a crucial element in bearing the burdens of another.

   c) Encouragement

   Those facing temptation need lots of encouragement. You might consider writing them, giving them study material, or teaching them.

   d) Comfort

   Paul said to the Corinthians that "God, who comforts the depressed, comforted us by the coming of Titus; and not only by his coming, but also by the comfort with which he was comforted in you" (2 Cor. 7:6-7). Paul fell to the flesh. But the comfort of fellowship and the presence of others uplifted his spirit.

3. What to avoid

   a) Being self-righteous

   Galatians 6:3 says, "If anyone thinks he is something when he is nothing, he deceives himself." At times we don't support stumbling believers because we feel superior to them. A lot of people like to look down on those in sin. They see someone in sin and they look down on them with a smug, self-righteous attitude.

I was touched by what one writer said of his own experience. It went something like this: "I've often thought that if I ever fall into a trespass, I will pray that I don't land in the hands of censorious, critical, self-righteous judges in the church. I'd rather fall into the hands of barkeepers, streetwalkers, or dope peddlers because such church people would tear me apart with their long wagging gossipy tongues, cutting me to shreds."

b) Being judgmental

A judgmental attitude is wrong. When you are judgmental, you are deceived; you are assuming you're something when you are really nothing on your own (Gal. 6:3). It's the Spirit in us that makes us or what we do worthwhile.

c) Being proud

If you don't want to get involved with stumbling believers because you think you're too good for that, you again are deceiving yourself. Instead, you had better go back and examine your own work to see if you have a just cause for boasting (v. 4). You'd better not assume anything that isn't really true. Your first responsibility is to examine your own life and be sure that your attitudes are right, that you have a humble spirit, and that you are boasting because of what God has done in your life. Then you will realize you are nothing apart from the power of the Spirit, and you will be able to help stumbling believers.

d) Being quick to compare

Verse 5 adds that "each one shall bear his own load." That doesn't contradict verse 2. The words translated "load" (v. 5) and "burdens" (v. 2) are different. "Burdens" (Gk., *baros*) speaks of a heavy burden, whereas "load" (Gk., *phortion*) refers to the general obligations of life.

96

Everyone is responsible to take care of his own life without comparing himself to others. If you compare yourself to God rather than to those around you, you'll be less likely to set yourself up as too superior to bend to the need of a sinner.

C. Build Them Up (v. 6)

"Let the one who is taught the word share all good things with him who teaches."

1. The meaning

This is not saying that preachers are to be paid. The context of the passage requires a different meaning. It is referring to a spiritual person who has come alongside to help a fleshly person. In that process, the spiritual person is obviously teaching the Word to the fleshly person. But the fleshly person isn't to be the only beneficiary of the relationship. He is to mutually share (Gk., *koinōneō*) with his spiritual helper in all "good things" (Gk., *agathoi*, "all noble, spiritual, and moral excellencies"). A relationship of restoration is to be of mutual spiritual benefit.

2. The message

This is a picture of the building that takes place in the restoration process. First there is a confrontation of sin— a call for confession, repentance, prayer, and a return to the standard of Scripture. Then the spiritual person holds the fallen brother accountable as he assists in carrying the burden of temptation. Finally, both are built up and edified as they share all the excellent moral truths that flow out of the teaching process.

3. The method

The building process could occur through sharing books, tapes, fellowship in church, and Bible study. Whatever the method, there must be a personal and mutually beneficial sharing of spiritual truths between the spiritual and fleshly person. True restoration requires both confrontation and a relationship that promotes holiness.

Conclusion

We are our brother's keeper. Not fulfilling our responsibility to restore fallen fellow believers is a serious error. We must be sensitive to one another's needs. Because we occasionally give in to the flesh, God has ordained that we be accountable to one another in the church. Therefore the Spirit directs those who are walking in the Spirit to participate in the ministry of restoration.

Focusing in the Facts

1. Can the Christian life be lived on an individual basis? Why or why not (see pp. 84-85)?
2. When do Christians grow spiritually (see p. 85)?
3. When a Christian is fleshly, what happens to his usefulness to God (see p. 85)?
4. Corporate ministry requires individual _____ (see p. 86).
5. If a church does not engage in the ministry of restoration, what happens to the believer's motivation to live a holy life (see p. 86)?
6. Who in the church has the responsibility to pick up the fleshly from their sin (Gal. 6:1; see p. 87)?
7. What characterizes those who are called to help the fleshly (see pp. 89-90)?
8. Is a Spirit-filled life something that is felt only? Explain (see p. 90).
9. When you are spiritual, are you perfect? Explain (see p. 90).
10. What procedure is used in the process of spiritual restoration (see pp. 90-92)?
11. During the process of restoration, what attitude is the spiritual man supposed to have toward the one being restored (see p. 92)?
12. Does the process of restoration end with confrontation? Explain (see pp. 93-94).
13. How do the spiritual bear the burdens of the fleshly (see p. 95)?
14. What kinds of attitudes must the spiritual avoid with respect to the fleshly (Gal. 6:3-5; see pp. 95-97)?
15. In building the fleshly person up, what kind of relationship is required between the spiritual and the fleshly (Gal. 6:6; see p. 97)?

Pondering the Principles

1. The church of our day is painfully aware of the devastating effect of uncorrected sin on the corporate Body. When the church tolerates individual believers who claim the name of Christ but live like the world, the light of the church begins to fade. Yet it is strange that someone who truly knows Christ would behave like an unbeliever. The Puritan pastor John Owen wrote that believers "find that sin . . . fills them with shame, self-abhorrence, and deep abasement of soul. They discern in . . . themselves on account of it, an unsuitableness to the holiness of God, and an unfitness for communion with him. Nothing do they more earnestly seek in prayer than a cleansing from it by the blood of Christ; not are any promises more precious to them, than those of purification from it" (*The Holy Spirit: His Gifts and Power*, George Burder, ed. [Grand Rapids: Kregel, 1954], p. 255). Believers—although not perfect—have an abhorrence of sin. Are you concerned that Christ's church be purified from sin? What effort, in the power of the Spirit and under the guidance of God's Word, are you going to make in your life so that you can be an agent for restoring others from sin?

2. Another Puritan pastor, Matthew Mead, wrote that "a Christian is universal in his obedience. He doth not obey one command and neglect another, do one duty and cast off another; but he hath respect to all the commands: he endeavours to leave every sin, and love every duty" (*The Almost Christian Discovered* [Beaver Falls, Pa.: Soli Deo Gloria Publications, n.d.], p. 174). The spiritual are to help the fleshly not only to avoid open sin but to be consistent in avoiding hidden sin. But that can be accomplished only when believers are involved in each other's lives. What effort will you make to be involved in the lives of fellow believers so that you can help them "leave every sin, and love every duty"? Are there believers involved in your life who can do the same thing for you?

Scripture Index

Topical Index

Accountability, importance of 94-95, 99

Addiction. *See* Drinking, Drugs

Alcohol. *See* Drinking

Augustine, Saint, his reliance on God, 40

Bearing burdens. *See* Restoration, ministry of

Body, the. *See* Flesh

Bridge, William, on faith as our remedy, 81

Bunyan, John
on the dusty room in *The Pilgrim's Progress*, 75
on Shameful in *The Pilgrim's Progress*, 19

Calvin, John, on the Holy Spirit's help, 59

Carroll, Joseph, experience of, 37-38, 47-48

Charismatic movement, the misrepresentations by, 9-10
overemphasis on the miraculous by, 10

Church
discipline. *See* Restoration, ministry of
growth, 12
ministry. *See* Spiritual gifts
programs, 11-12

Conviction. *See* Holy Spirit

Counseling
biblical, 14, 34, 56-57
divine, 45-46
family, 79
marital, 79

overemphasis on, 11-17, 67, 71-72, 79-80
professional, 56-57, 79

Death, dealing with a spouse's, 40-41

Depression, 56, 79. *See also* Counseling

Despair, 56. *See also* Counseling

Discernment, importance of, 34

Discipline, church. *See* Restoration, ministry of

Discouragement, 56, 64. *See also* Counseling

Drinking
dealing with an addiction, 56-57
sins associated with, 77

Drugs
dealing with an addiction, 56-57
sins associated with, 77

Evangelism, methods of, 24, 59-60

Family, counseling. *See* Counseling

Flesh, the
dealing with, 74-76, 78-80
deeds of, 76-77
definition of, 72-74
sanctification and. *See* Sanctification

God
access to, 26-29, 33-34
de-emphasis on. *See* Pragmatism

intimacy with. *See* access to
power of, 58-59
provision of, 38-40
sovereignty of, 12-13

Holy Spirit, the
access to God through. *See*
God
baptism of, 25
Christ-centeredness of, 41-44,
48
conviction by. *See* saving
work of
de-emphasis on, 8-19
fruit of, 78
gifts of. *See* Spiritual gifts
grieving, 68
guidance by. *See* leading of
illumination by. *See*
Illumination
indwelling of, 25
intercession by, 60-62
internal work of, 10
leading of, 44-46
listening to, 54
ministries of, 21-64, 68
miraculous works of, 10
misrepresentations of, 9-10
power of. *See* strengthening
by
quenching, 68
regeneration by. *See* saving
work of
repentance by. *See* saving
work of
salvation and. *See* saving
work of
sanctifying work of, 8-19, 25-
26. *See also* ministries of
saving work of, 23-24, 67
Scripture and, 31-32
seal of, 26
strengthening by, 57-60

sufficiency of, 32-33, 36, 45-46,
50-52, 62, 81
walking by, 65-99
Humanism. *See* Pragmatism

Illumination
definition of, 30, 34
descriptions of, 30-31
Immorality, sexual. *See* Sexual
immorality
Inadequacy. *See*
Discouragement
Insecurity. *See* Discouragement

Jesus Christ
glorifying. *See* Holy Spirit
Holy Spirit's relation to. *See*
Holy Spirit
preciousness of, 43

Lloyd-Jones, Martyn, on the
plight of man, 18

Man
depravity of, 13, 18, 22-23
overemphasis on. *See*
Pragmatism
plight of. *See* depravity of
Marriage, counseling. *See*
Counseling
Mead, Matthew, on universal
obedience, 99
Ministry, mutual. *See* Spiritual
gifts
Moses, insecurity of, 64
Mutual ministry. *See* Spiritual
gifts

"One anothers" of Scripture,
55. *See also* Spiritual gifts
Owen, John, on the believer's
hatred of sin, 99